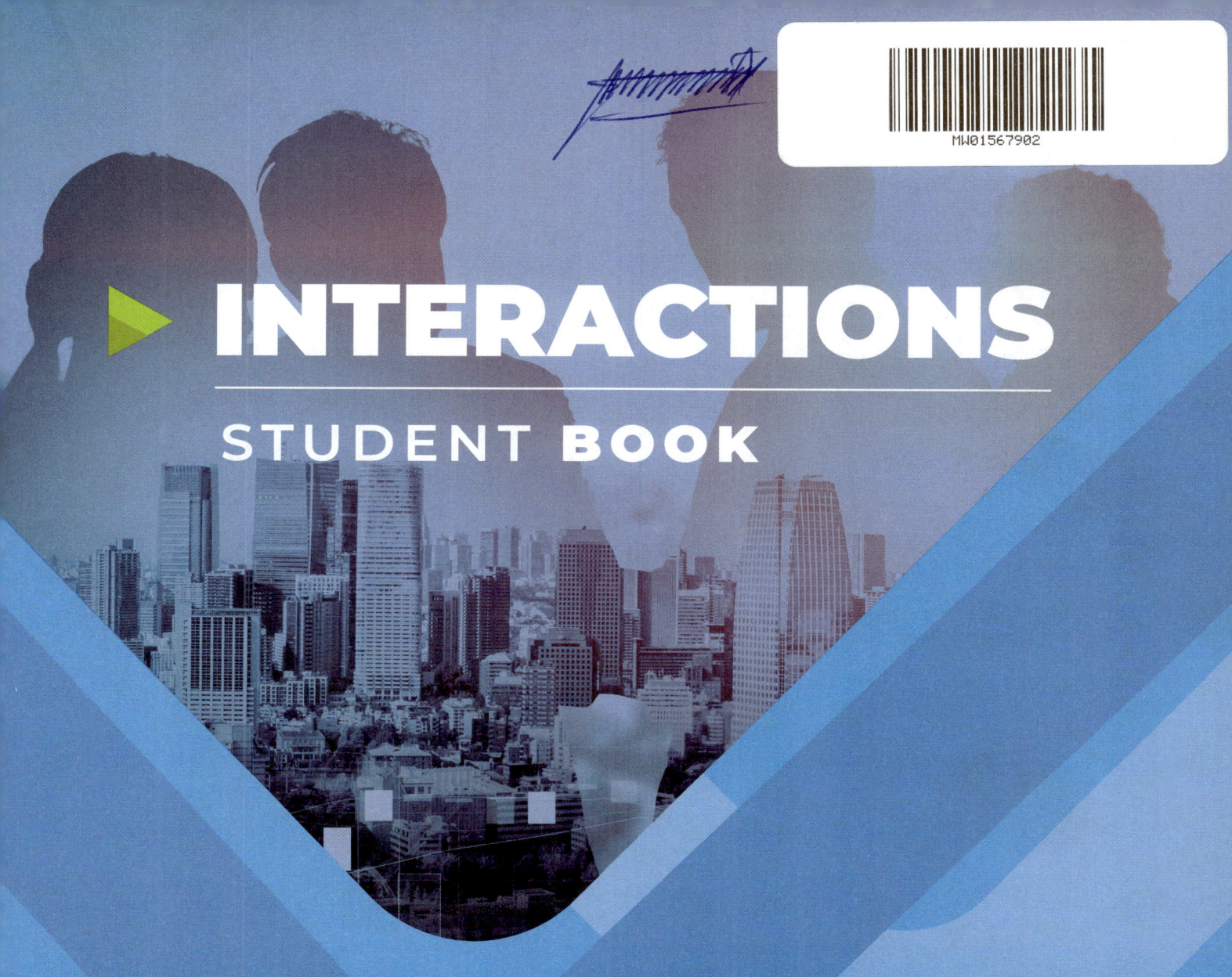

Copyright © 2008 by Uceda International, Inc.
All rights reserved. No part of this book
may be reproduced in any form or
by any means without permission in writing
from the publisher.

Printed in the United States of America.

Published by Uceda International
New Jersey, USA
Second Edition - 2022

ISBN : 978-1-935318-37-8

Collaboration:

Text, Grammar and Readings:	Alexa Germosen and Brauny Gonzalez

Front and back cover design,	- Elizabeth García
graphic design and illustrations:	- Victoria Da Silva

Table of Contents

UNIT 1 3
Although / In Spite of / Despite / Though
So / Such
Present Perfect Tense - Review
Ever / Never / Already / Yet / Before
Still / Anymore

UNIT 2 23
Reported Speech
Say vs. Tell
Indirect Commands
Reported Speech / Questions with "if"
Reported Speech / Wh- Questions
Phrasal Verbs

UNIT 3 41
Will vs. Going to
Relative Clauses
Whatever / Whoever / Wherever / Whenever

UNIT 4 59
Noun Clauses with "If"
Noun Clauses with a Question Word
Directions
Another One/ The Other One
Others / The Others

UNIT 5 75
Adjectives and Adverbs
Adverbs of Manner
Adverbs of Frequency

UNIT 6 95
Comparative Adjectives
Short Answers with Infinitives
Adjectives Followed by Infinitives

UNIT 7 115
Gerunds
Superlative Form of Adjectives and Adverbs

UNIT 8 131
Tag Questions
Causative Verbs
Verbs of Perception

UNIT 9 149
Adjectives Ending in -ED & -ING
Synonyms
Antonyms

UNIT 10 165
Tense Discrimination
Tense Usage
Review of Verbs

APPENDIX 181
200 Irregular Verbs
Common Separable Phrasal Verbs
Common Nonseparable Phrasal Verbs
Common Verbs Followed by Gerunds
Common Verbs Followed by Infinitives
Common Verbs Followed by Gerunds or Infinitives

Preface

Interactions is an intermediate grammar and conversation textbook in the UCEDA series. Its main focus is to review some of the grammatical structures presented in previous levels with the idea of reinforcing and further ingraining grammar concepts easily forgotten by ESL students. Furthermore, the text introduces, drills and reinforces certain types of grammar not readily found in other textbooks of its kind. The book also introduces new and advanced concepts of grammar in preparation for subsequent levels.

The text consists of 36 lessons in 10 units. The units are not put in a specific order, allowing the instructor the flexibility to teach the units in the order that may best suit the needs of the students. Although the length of each unit is pretty much consistent throughout the entire book, the number of topics in each unit varies depending on the subject matter at hand.

Each unit contains introductory warm up readings and dialogues, a grammar focus for each topic and plenty of written exercises. Guided conversations in each unit promote oral practice. Units also contain pronunciation sections that improve students' English accent through the implementation of the linking effect, thought provoking readings to stimulate conversation and debate, and creative writing activities for students to express themselves on paper.

Although there is no prescribed methodology for presenting the material in this book, its format can support a number of approaches. The text, however, follows a standard format of warm up, grammar presentation and written and oral exercises. Exercises consist of sentence completion drills, fill-in-the-blank activities and identification and transformation tasks. Units also feature occasional repetition of expressions and grammar usage from previous lessons in order to help the student retain them.

Units one, two, three and *seven* contain reviews of the present perfect tense, phrasal verbs, future tense and verbs plus infinitive or gerunds respectively.

Units five, six and *seven* deal with adjectives and adverbs in their different forms.

Unit four is of special interest since it deals with the functional aspect of embedded questions, as in when asking for directions.

Unit eight deals with less challenging aspects of grammar such as tag questions and causative verbs.

Units nine and *ten* deal with adjectives with special endings, tense discrimination and a review of verbs.

The book contains a comprehensive appendix that lists 200 irregular verbs in their present, past and past participle forms, an extensive list of phrasal verbs and verbs that are followed by infinitives, gerunds or both.

It has been the ultimate purpose of the writers, collaborators and researchers of this book to address concerns and problem areas often encountered by ESL students at this level of instruction. They trust that its content will more than adequately prepare students to overcome those difficulties. It is the genuine hope of the authors that this book becomes an invaluable asset to students and teachers alike and their belief that the adequate implementation of its material will greatly enhance the effectiveness of any curriculum. Ultimately, all those involved in the creation of this book would like to thank their pupils, without whom this book would not have been possible. This book was created because of them and for them.

UNIT 1

Content

- Although / In Spite of / Despite / Though
- So / Such
- Present Perfect Tense - Review
- Ever / Never / Already / Yet / Before
- Still / Anymore

> **Although** Mary was sad, she smiled

01. COMMUNICATION **02. COMPREHENSION** **03. WRITING** **04. GRAMMAR**

Unit 1

Young at Heart

Reading

Although my parents are not young, they're very energetic people.

Last year, they spent their summer vacation at a beach resort in the Caribbean. The main attraction there was the practice of extreme sports.

In spite of the fact that both my parents are over sixty years old, they registered to participate in most of the sports activities organized by the resort, such as: *scuba diving, *rappelling and *hang-gliding, just to mention some of them.

Despite the occasional rain, they enjoyed their vacation a lot and promised to go back every year.

"After all," my father said, "you only live once, and though we might not be young anymore, we'll always be **young at heart**."

* **hang-gliding**: *the sport of launching oneself from a cliff by means of a kitelike v-shaped wing*
* **rappelling**: *the action of moving down a vertical face of a mountain by means of a double rope secured to the body*
* **scuba diving**: *to dive underwater through the use of a breathing device strapped to the back of the diver*

Comprehension Questions

Answer true, false or maybe.

1. My parents are old, but energetic. _____
2. Extreme sports can be dangerous. _____
3. Both my parents like to practice extreme sports. _____
4. You need a breathing device to do rappelling. _____
5. It didn't rain on their vacation. _____
6. They promised to come back next year. _____

Grammar Focus

ALTHOUGH / IN SPITE OF / DESPITE / THOUGH

Although + (subject + verb + complement)

- Although it rained occasionally, my parents enjoyed their vacation.
- She didn't get tired although she was working really hard.

In spite of or *Despite* + (noun, a pronoun [that/what/this, etc.], or –ing).

- In spite of the rain, they enjoyed their vacation.
- She didn't get the promotion in spite of being extremely qualified for it.

Despite is the same as *in spite of*; however, notice that we do not use the preposition "of" after despite.

- In spite of being extremely qualified for the position, she didn't get it.
- She didn't get the position despite being extremely qualified for it.

Compare *although* and *in spite of/despite*

- Although Mary was sad, she smiled.
- In spite of her sadness, she smiled.
- Despite her sadness, she smiled.

Sometimes we use *though* instead of *although*:

- I didn't get the job though I had the qualifications.

Note: In spoken English, we often use **though** at the end of the sentence meaning "but." Note that you put a comma before "though" when it is at the end of a sentence.

The house isn't very big. It has a big garden, **though**. (= but it has a big garden)
I see her every day. I've never spoken to her, though. (= but I've never spoken to her)

Unit 1

Exercise 1.1

Complete the sentences. Use Although + a sentence from the box.

> I'd been there twice before.
> It was pretty hot.
> He had studied a lot.
> We planned everything carefully.
> I was really tired.
> The weather was terrible.
>
> I didn't speak French.
> We don't like him very much.
> My ankle was injured.
> It rained.
> I had a big breakfast.
> I don't like big cities.

Example: *Although there was a lot of noise, I managed to get to sleep.*

1. _____, we thought we'd better invite him to the party.
2. _____, I managed to make myself understood.
3. _____, I didn't recognize the restaurant at first.
4. _____, I had to walk back home.
5. _____, she was wearing a heavy coat.
6. _____, he didn't pass the test.
7. _____, we still went to the annual company picnic.
8. _____, the surprise party was a big mess.
9. _____, we managed to drive home safely.
10. _____, I had to move to New York City.
11. _____, I couldn't fall asleep.
12. _____, I was starving by the time lunch was served.

Unit 1

Exercise 1.2

Make one sentence from two. Use the word(s) in parentheses in your sentences.

Example:

The day was beautiful. We spent the whole day indoors. (despite)
Despite the beautiful day, we spent the whole day indoors.

1. I didn't eat anything. I was very hungry. (in spite of)

   _____.

2. She accepted the job. The salary was low. (despite)

   _____.

3. I went to work. I was still feeling sick. (although)

   _____.

4. We planned everything. A lot of things went wrong. (despite)

   _____.

5. I couldn't sleep. I was tired. (although)

   _____.

6. We went out. The rain was very heavy. (despite)

   _____.

7. She speaks English well. We couldn't understand her. (although)

   _____.

8. We enjoyed our vacation. The weather was terrible. (in spite of)

   _____.

9. I was exhausted. I couldn't fall asleep. (although)

   _____.

10. I like Ann. She's very selfish. (although)

    _____.

Unit 1

The Date

Reading

A few days after meeting Jane, Karl calls her for a date.

Karl: Hi, Jane, this is Karl.
Jane: Karl, how are you?
Karl: I'm fine. Listen, are you doing anything this afternoon?
Jane: No, I'm not. I don't have any plans.
Karl: Well... I was wondering, since it's such a beautiful afternoon, would you like to go downtown with me? There's a new outdoor café on Park Avenue.
Jane: I'd love to go. I heard it's such a nice place and that the food is very good. Actually, some of my friends from school will also be there this afternoon.
Karl: Really? Maybe going to the new café is not such a good idea after all!

Comprehension Questions

1. What's a date?
2. Have you ever dated anyone from a different race, culture, etc? Explain.
3. What's an outdoor café?
4. How does Karl feel about Jane's friends?
5. Are they still going to go out?

Unit 1

Grammar Focus

SO and SUCH

We use SO and SUCH to emphasize an adjective or adverb or to make its meaning stronger.

We use so + adjective/adverb:

so big   so quickly
so nice   so enjoyable

- I really liked the movie. The story was **so nice**.
- New York city is **so big**. It scares me to go there by myself.
- Nick is a great athlete. He runs **so quickly**.

We use such + noun:

Such a fool   such angels   such a liar

We also use such + a + adjective + noun (singular) AND such + adjective + noun (plural)

such a nice movie   such nice people

- I really enjoyed the party. The Smiths are **such nice people**.
- It was **such a nice movie**. I'll probably watch it again.

More examples:
- It's such a beautiful day, isn't it? It's so warm. (= really warm)
- We enjoyed our vacation. We had such a good time. (= a really good time)

You can use: so............that......   - The box was <u>so</u> heavy <u>that</u> I had to put it down.
               such..........that......   - It was <u>such</u> a nice party <u>that</u> we stayed up until 2:00 a.m.

We also use so and such to mean "like this"

- His room was so messy. I've never seen such a mess. (= a mess like this)

Note that we also say: A. "**so** long" but "**such** a long time"
                         B. "**so** far" but "**such** a long way"

Unit 1

Exercise 1.3

Change the sentences using "such."

> **Example :** *Ana is so beautiful. Ana is such a beautiful lady.*

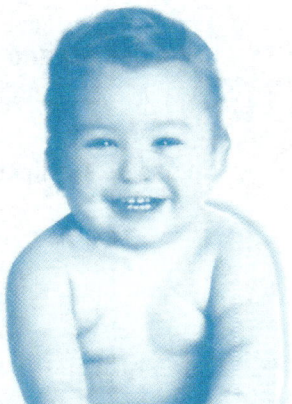

1. The boy is so tall. He is _____.
2. That watch is so pretty. That is _____.
3. The baby is so beautiful. He is _____.
4. The car is so expensive. It is_____.
5. Today is so cold. It is _____.
6. They are so humble. They're_____.
7. You're so special. You're _____.
8. The policeman is so grouchy. He is_____.
9. This milk is so healthy. This is _____.
10. My boss is so busy. He is_____.

Exercise 1.4

A. Change the following sentences using "so."

1. This is such a pretty picture. This picture is _____.
2. Those are such heavy boxes. Those boxes are_____.
3. This is such a dirty table. This table is _____.
4. Mr. Chin is such a busy man. Mr. Chin is _____.
5. John is such an honest guy. John is _____.
6. Bob is such a kind person. Bob is_____.
7. Martha is such a sweet girl. Martha is_____.
8. Jenny is such a stupid girl. Jenny is _____.
9. This is such an interesting book. This book is_____.
10. This is such an easy lesson. This lesson is_____.

B. Complete with "so," "such," "such a," or "such an."

1. David is _____ tired today.
2. Annie looked_____ beautiful last night.

Unit 1

3. They are _____ rich people.
4. This is _____ interesting book.
5. Michael and Cindy are _____ talented children.
6. She's _____ nice doctor.
7. Today is _____ cold.
8. Those are _____ interesting stories.
9. I'm _____ excited and I can't hide it.
10. This is _____ delicious wine.
11. Manuel is _____ liar.
12. This is _____ good idea.
13. You're _____ good friend.
14. Kevin is _____ conceited.
15. I'm _____ smart girl.

C. Complete the sentences using "so...that..."

> **Examples:** I'm <u>so</u> hungry <u>that I could eat a horse</u>.
> Harry was <u>so</u> nervous <u>that he forgot his lines</u>.

1. Rachel was so scared _____.
2. Linda was so tired _____.
3. Our teacher was so angry _____.
4. I'm so mad right now _____.
5. This coffee is so hot _____.

D. Complete the sentences using "such...that..."

> **Examples:** My boss is <u>such</u> a nice person <u>that he never gets mad when we're late</u>.
> My grandmother is <u>such</u> an educated woman <u>that she never raises her voice</u>.

1. I was having such a good time at the party _____.
2. She's such a rich woman _____.
3. My father had such an interesting life _____.
4. Titanic was such an interesting movie _____.
5. That was such a long book _____.

Unit 1

You're a real go-getter.

Reading

James: Hi, Lisa. How've you been?
Lisa: Fine. What about you?
James: Everything's fine with me, too.
Lisa: It's nice to hear that.
James: Where are you going?
Lisa: I'm going over to Paul's. How about you?
James: I'm going to the library to borrow some books. I have to study for an important test tomorrow.
Lisa: Really? I didn't know you were going to school. What are you studying?
James: I'm studying computer science.
Lisa: How long have you been studying computer science?
James: I've been studying it since last year. What about you? Are you attending any school?
Lisa: Actually, I haven't attended school since I graduated from high school in 1999. I'm currently working as a secretary for an important law firm.
James: How long have you been working there?
Lisa: For about a year. What about you? Are you still working at the bank?
James: Yeah. I've been working there for five years and I also have a part-time job at a lawyer's office.
Lisa : Wow! You're a real go-getter. Well, James, I really have to get going now. It was nice seeing you again.
James: It was nice to see you, too. Maybe we could get together sometime.
Lisa: That sounds good. Take care.
James: Bye.

I am a go-getter.
I am for success!!

Unit 1

Exercise 1.5

Read the information about James and Lisa. Then circle the letter of the sentence that best describes the situation.

1. James has studied computer science since last year.
   a. He is still studying.
   b. He is not studying anymore.

2. Lisa hasn't attended any school since she graduated from high school in 1999.
   a. She was in high school in 1999.
   b. She is in high school now.

3. James has worked at a bank for five years.
   a. He got the job at the bank five years ago and still works there.
   b. He got the job five years ago, but doesn't work there anymore.

4. Lisa has worked as a secretary for a law firm for a year.
   a. She began to work there as a secretary a year ago.
   b. She didn't begin to work there as a secretary a year ago.

Exercise 1.6

Present Perfect Tense Review
Complete the following conversations using Present Perfect Tense and the verb in parentheses.

1. A: _____ you ever _____ Japanese food? (eat)

   B: Yes, I _____.

2. A: How long _____ you _____ a teacher? (be)

   B: Well, I _____ a teacher since 1990.

3. A: Can I throw this newspaper away?

   B: No, I _____ it yet. (read)

4. A: How many games _____ the Yankees _____ so far? (win)

   B: I think they _____ three games.

5. A: John, don't forget we have to pay the phone and cable bills.

   B: Well, I _____ already _____ the phone bill, but I _____ the cable bill yet. (pay)

Unit 1

6. A: Would you like some chocolate?
   B: No, thanks. I _____ already _____ five cups. (drink)

7. A: _____ Arnold _____ his new car yet? (drive)
   B: Yes, he has. He drove it yesterday.

8. A: _____ you _____ Lisa about our plans? (tell)
   B: No, I _____ her anything yet.

9. A: My friend Kevin _____ a new house. (buy)
   B: Good for him! I'm very happy to hear that.

10. A: How long _____ Fred _____ that car? (have)
    B: He _____ it for a long time.

11. A: Mary, how long _____ we _____ together? (be)
    B: We _____ together for so long that I lost count, sweetie.

Grammar Review

These time expressions are used with the Present Perfect Tense to indicate past actions when a precise time is not stated.

EVER / NEVER	ALREADY / YET / NOT...YET
I - Ever is used in questions and has the meaning of **"at any time in a person's life."** Its position is before the past participle. - Have you **ever** been to Japan? - Has Lisa **ever** eaten lobster?	**I - Already** is used in affirmative sentences and has the meaning of **"previously"** or **"before the time of speaking."** Its position is before the past participle. - I've **already** done my homework. - She's **already** finished the test.
II - Never is used in negative statements and it means **"at no point in a person's life."** Its position is before the past participle. - I have **never** been to such beautiful place! - Tom has **never** driven a truck.	**II - Yet (interrogative):** Yet is used in questions and it is placed at the end. - Have you finished your homework **yet**? - Has he packed his bags **yet**? **Yet (negative):** Yet is used in negative statements and it means **"up to now"** or **"so far."** - We haven't called them **yet**. - She has not made a decision **yet**.

The preposition **"before"** is often used with both **"ever"** and **"never"** with the meaning of "before now." It's placed at the end of the sentence.

A: Have you ever seen her **before**?
B: No, I've never seen her **before**.

Unit 1

Exercise 1.7

Complete the following sentences using YET/ALREADY/EVER/NEVER and BEFORE. Use the correct form of the verb in parentheses.

1. She has already (do) <u>done</u> this kind of job <u>before</u>.
2. I haven't (send)_____ the mail _____.
3. We have _____(speak) _____ about the contract.
4. He has _____(eat) _____ meat in his life.
5. Have you _____(feed) _____ a baby before?
6. Have you _____ (tell) _____ them about your new job?
7. It's getting late. Have you (finish) _____ your homework _____?
8. I haven't (meet)_____ your wife _____.
9. Have you _____ (be) _____ to Mexico?
10. The teacher has _____(be) _____ late to class.

Exercise 1.8

Rewrite the sentences using "already" or "yet." Put the sentences in Present Perfect Tense.

> **Example:**
>
> I finished my homework one hour ago.
>
> *In other words*, I have **already** finished my homework.

1. Mary didn't finish her work yesterday. She's doing it right now.

    In other words, _____.

2. We studied the past tense last week.

    In other words, _____.

3. We started this exercise five minutes ago.

    In other words, _____.

4. We began chapter 8 three days ago. We haven't finished it.

    In other words,_____.

5. Susan has been working at the drugstore for over five years now. She still works there.

   In other words, _____.

6. I expected Ted to come one hour ago, but he didn't come.

   In other words, _____.

7. My brother stopped smoking five years ago.

   In other words, _____.

8. I was hungry one hour ago. I ate a sandwich.

   In other words, _____.

9. I started a letter to my parents yesterday. I'm still writing it.

   In other words, _____.

10. I don't have to study tonight. I studied yesterday.

    In other words, _____.

11. I began to read the newspaper at 8:00. I finished reading it an hour ago.

    In other words, _____.

12. I get home at 10:45 p.m. My children go to bed at 10:00 p.m. every night.

    In other words, _____.

Unit 1

Grammar Focus

STILL / ANYMORE

STILL

- We use **still** to say that a situation or action is continuing. It hasn't changed or stopped.

   - It's 10:00 and Tom is **still** in bed.
   - When I went to bed, you were **still** watching TV.
   - Does she **still** want to come to the party with us?

- **Still** usually goes in the middle of the sentence by the verb.

ANYMORE

- We use **not.......anymore** or **not..........any longer** to say that a situation has changed. **Anymore** and **any longer** go at the end of the sentence:

   - Mary does **not** live here **anymore** (or **any longer**). She moved two months ago.
   - We used to work together, but we <u>don't</u> **anymore** (or **any longer**).

- You can also use **no longer**. **No longer** goes in the middle of the sentence:

   - Mary **no longer** lives here.

Compare **still** and **not...... anymore:**   - Sara **still** lives here, but Mary <u>doesn't</u> live here **anymore**.

Exercise 1.9

Compare what Mike said a few years ago with what he says now. Some things are the same as before, but some things have changed.

I work in a gas station.
I want to be a lawyer.
I'm single.
I go surfing a lot.
I'm interested in politics.
I go dancing a lot.

Mike a few years ago

I work for a law firm.
I graduated as a lawyer last year.
I'm married.
I gave up surfing.
I'm not interested in politics.
I go dancing a lot.

Mike now

A- Write sentences about Mike using "still" and "not...anymore." Use the words in parentheses.

1. (work) _____.
2. (lawyer) _____.
3. (single) _____.
4. (surfing) _____.
5. (politics) _____.
6. (dancing) _____.

B- Now write four sentences about Mike using "no longer."

Example: *He no longer works at a gas station.*

1. _____.
2. _____.
3. _____.
4. _____.

Exercise 1.10

Two people are talking about the place where they live. Write replies using *still* or *not.....anymore*.

A: There was a beautiful park.
B: Well, the park is still beautiful.
A: Children used to play on the streets.
B: Not now. They don't play on the streets anymore.

Old Man:

1. People could go out late at night.
2. There were green fields everywhere.
3. Streets were clean.
4. The river was crystal blue.
5. The view from Chapel Hill was breathtaking.
6. People were polite and friendly.
7. It was our home.

Young Man:

1. Well, _____.
2. I'm afraid _____.
3. Not now. _____.
4. I'm afraid _____.
5. Well, _____.
6. In a way, _____.
7. And _____.

Unit 1

 ## Guided Conversation

Using the model practice the use of STILL and ANYMORE.

Example:
(work at the gas station)
(work at the hospital)

A: Hi, _____ ! Do you still <u>work at the Gas Station</u>?
B: No, I don't <u>work there</u> anymore. What about you? Do you still <u>work at the hospital</u>?
A: Yes, I still <u>work there</u>.

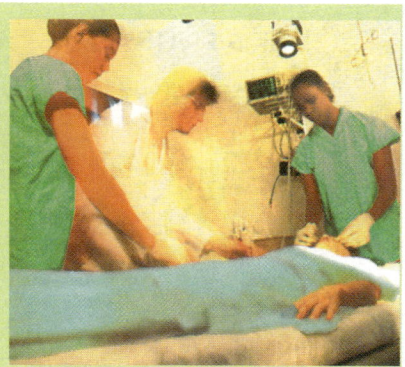

1. (play/tennis with your friends)
   (play/chess at the club)

2. (play/soccer on the weekend)
   (play/golf at the country club)

3. (live/874 Main street)
   (live/930 Broadway)

4. (be/a lawyer)
   (be/a teacher)

5. (go /Europe on vacation)
   (go/Egypt on vacation)

6. (be/married)
   (be/single)

7. (go/dancing every weekend)
   (go/fishing every weekend)

8. (interested/politics)
   (interested/astronomy)

9. (be/student)
   (be/teacher)

10. (On your own)

Unit 1

Pronunciation Section

Phonological Feature

> **LINKING WITH -ED**
> When a final **-ed** is followed by a vowel, the sounds are linked. The **-d** sounds like part of the next word.
> Example: They worked on Main Street.

Exercise 1.11

A. **Practice the following sentences.**

- The plane *arrived on* time.

- She *remembered us* from the party.

- I *parked on* Market Street.

- My sister *needed a* raise.

- They *lived on* Main Street for five years.

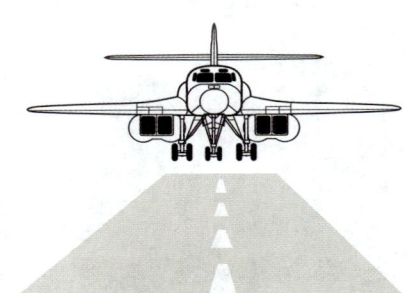

B. **Listen carefully to the audio program (or your teacher), and complete these sentences with the missing words. Mark the linking sound.**

1. Mr. Williams _____ _____ his new rain coat.

2. She _____ _____ new stereo.

3. He _____ _____ 7:00 yesterday.

4. Sheila _____ _____ new store last week.

5. They _____ _____ experienced person for the job.

Unit 1

Life's too short.

▲ Reading

Ever since I can remember, my friend Lucille has worked as a medical assistant at one of the best private medical centers in town. "Lucy," as she likes to be called, is so smart that she managed to finish college in less than three years.

By the time she was twenty-one years old, she had already graduated from college. She was so anxious to begin working that she got a part-time job as a home health aide, where she had to take care of sick people and assist them in their homes.

Lucy's life is never boring. She's always busy and she loves it. She knows that nowadays it is hard to find a good job and you need to have many skills in order to be hired. That's why she's preparing herself the best she can. As she puts it, "Life is too short, and you should not put off until tomorrow what you can do today."

Comprehension Questions

1. What kind of person do you think Lucy is?
2. Is she a negative person?
3. Why does she study hard?
4. What do you need in order to be hired for a job?
5. Is Lucy a boring person to be with?
6. How old were you when you finished college?
7. What are your future aspirations?
8. What's a workaholic?
9. Explain the last proverb. What does it mean?

Life is too short to postpone things.

Unit 1

Writing

Using the paragraph from the first page of the unit as a model, write a composition about your parents. You can include real or fictitious information.

Remember to use :

Although
Even though
In spite of
Despite, etc.
So and *such* to emphasize adjectives

You can start your composition like this:

Although my parents are...

UNIT 2

Content

- Reported Speech
- Say vs. Tell
- Indirect Commands
- Reported Speech / Questions with "if"
- Reported Speech / Wh- Questions
- Phrasal Verbs

"She **said** that she **was** busy"

01. COMMUNICATION   02. COMPREHENSION   03. WRITING   04. GRAMMAR

Unit 2

Did you get my messages?

Reading

It's Carmen's first day at work. Her boss just got back from lunch, and he's asking her about his messages.

Mr. Hiroki: Hi, Carmen! I'm back.
Carmen: Hello, Mr. Hiroki. How did your business lunch go?
Mr. Hiroki: It went just fine, thank you. The investors said that they were very happy with our product.
Carmen: I'm really happy to hear that.
Mr. Hiroki: Do I have any messages?
Carmen: Yes, sir. In fact, several people called while you were out to lunch. Mr. Smith from the insurance company called. He said that he would call back later. Mrs. Wilkins from the bank called. She said that your checkbooks would be ready by Monday.
Mr. Hiroki: Did my wife call?
Carmen: Yes, she did. She said that she had lost her car keys and wanted you to call her back as soon as you got here.
Mr. Hiroki: Thank you. Is that it?
Carmen: I almost forgot. Your friend Dan came over and waited for a while. He told me that unfortunately he had to cancel his tennis game with you. He also said that he'd call you later.
Mr. Hiroki: Well, you have certainly been very busy on your first day at work!!

Comprehension Questions

1. How long has Carmen been working for Mr. Hiroki?
2. How do you think she feels in her new job?
3. What did Mr. Hiroki ask Carmen after coming back from lunch?
4. What did Mr. Smith say to Carmen?
5. What did the lady from the bank say?
6. Who else called?
7. What did the person tell Carmen?
8. What did Mr. Hiroki's friend say to her?

Unit 2

Grammar Focus

| REPORTED SPEECH : | HE SAID THAT..... / HE TOLD ME THAT....... |

 *I'm Italian.*

He said that he was Italian.

 *I've been to Paris three times!*

She told me that she had been to Paris three times.

Am/is → was	(she said) "I'm busy." → She said that she was busy. (they said to us) "The movie isn't very good." → They told us that the movie wasn't very good.
Are → were	(I said) "The flowers are beautiful." → I said that the flowers were beautiful.
Have/has → had	(He said to me) "I've been here for two days." → He told me that he had been here for two days.
Can → could	(Mark said) "I can't ride a horse." → Mark said that he couldn't ride a horse.
Will → would	(my doctor said to me) "The exam will be easy." → My doctor told me that the exam would be easy.
Do/does → did	(I said) "It doesn't matter." → I said that it didn't matter. (He said) "I don't have your phone number." → He said that he didn't have my phone number.
Like → liked	(Sara said) "I like pizza." → Sara said that she liked pizza.
Go → went	(they said) "We go to the beach every weekend." → They said that they went to the beach every weekend.
Must → had to	(he said) "I must study hard to get good grades. → He said that he had to study hard to get good grades.
May → might	(they said) "We may stay until the end of the game." → They said that they might stay until the end of the game.
Went → had gone	(she said) "I went to the party." → She said that she had gone to the party.

* Reported speech refers to reproducing the idea of another person's words. Not all of the exact words are used: Verb forms and pronouns may change. Quotation marks are not used.

Unit 2

Exercise 2.1

Change the Quoted Speech to Reported Speech. Change the verb in the Quoted Speech to a form in Reported Speech as appropriate.

1. My father said, "I'm starving." _____.
2. Rita said, "I don't like boxing."_____.
3. Joe said, "I am planning a surprise party."_____.
4. Fred said, "I really love dancing."_____.
5. Kate said, "I called my mother today."_____.
6. Mr. Charles said, "I've already eaten lunch today."_____.
7. Hugo said, "I must visit my mother more often."_____.
8. Eric said, "I will come to the party."_____.
9. Jean said, "I can't afford to buy a new car." _____.
10. Mrs. Young said, "I must talk to my boss today."_____.
11. My teacher said, "You have a test next week." _____.
12. My father said, " You're too young to drive."_____.

Exercise 2.2 Oral

Change the sentences to Reported Speech.

1. "I don't get mad." (Rita)
2. "I want to have a Caesar salad." (Jessie)
3. "I don't want to eat home fries. I want to eat French fries." (the girl)
4. "Our mother passed away." (they)
5. "We are not in the mood." (they)
6. "I wash my car on Saturdays." (Mr. Jones)
7. "My girlfriend isn't beautiful." (Andrew)
8. "I don't speak English well, but my sister does." (Kim)
9. "I must save more money." (Jim)
10. "I haven't studied, but Linda has." (Robert)
11. "My teacher thinks she is pretty." (Pablo)
12. "I didn't do the homework." (Mike)

Grammar Focus

USING SAY vs. TELL	
(a) Mary said **that** she was tired.	**SAY** is followed by a noun clause.
(b) Mary told **me that** she was tired. (c) Mary told **us that** she was tired. (d) Mary told **Peter that** she was tired. (e) Mary told **someone that** she was tired.	**Tell** is not followed immediately by a noun clause. **Tell** is followed immediately by an object pronoun (me, you, him, her, it, us, them), a proper name (John, Julio, Becky, Sarah) or a noun (children, bus) **INCORRECT:** Mary told that she was tired. **CORRECT:** Mary told me that she was tired.

Exercise 2.3

Complete the following sentences with the correct form of Say or Tell.

1. Mr. Clark _____ his wife that he was excited about the trip.
2. Timmy _____ that he had to finish his homework.
3. Jean _____ me you were sick.
4. Did Peter _____ that he would be absent today?
5. She _____ she liked you.
6. The man_____ us he was a policeman.
7. Did they_____ you their names?
8. I _____ them it was very late.
9. He _____ me he was disappointed.
10. He _____ that he was happy.
11. They _____ they didn't want to work overtime.
12. Did they _____ you their address?

Exercise 2.4 Oral

Practice using told (someone) in Reported Speech.

Example: I need to talk to you.

Student A: (with book open, choose a sentence at random from the list on the next page and whisper to B.) - "I need to talk to you."

Student B: (with book closed, report to the group.)
- "(Liz) told me that she needed to talk to me".

Unit 2

I will call her tomorrow.
I don't know your sister.
I have never been to (Paris).
It's getting late.
I'm not married.
I like your sister/brother.

I think you speak English very well.
I won't be in class tomorrow.
I don't like today's weather.
I hate to get up early in the morning.
I'm going to take a vacation in (Florida)
I know how to dance (tango).

Grammar Focus

INDIRECT COMMANDS

Express orders or commands in Indirect Speech by using the infinitive form.

He said to me, "Come back in a week."
He told me **to come back** in a week.

She said to me, "Don't call me anymore."
She told me **not to call** her anymore.

Exercise 2.5

Change the following sentences to Indirect Commands. Use "told."

Example:
"Don't laugh at me," Paul said to Gina.
<u>Paul told Gina **not to** laugh at **him**.</u>

1. "Brush your teeth after every meal," Mary said to her son.
   _____.

2. "Wait for me," Mrs. Potter said to Sara.
   _____.

3. "Don't touch me," Rita said to Paul.
   _____.

4. "Hug me," Mark said to Stella.
   _____.

5. "Give me all your money," the thief said to Monica.
   _____.

Unit 2

6. "Come back," my sister said to her boyfriend.
   _____.

7. "Call me tonight," Nancy said to Peter.
   _____.

8. "Tell me the truth," Simon said to his girlfriend.
   _____.

9. "Kiss me," my mother said to my father.
   _____.

10. "Check the car's brakes," the mechanic said to his assistant.
    _____.

11. "Stop being stubborn," the wife said to her husband.
    _____.

12. "Don't play with my toys," little Jimmy said to his friend.
    _____.

Grammar Focus

REPORTED SPEECH : USING ASK IF in YES/NO QUESTIONS.	
Ask, -NOT say or tell- , is used to report a yes/no question	
YES/NO QUESTION Sara said to me, "Are you ready?" Sara said to Lisa, "Are you ready?"	**NOUN CLAUSE** (a) Sara **asked** me **if** I was ready. (b) Sara **asked** Lisa **if** she was ready.
Incorrect: Sara asked me that I was ready. **If,** not that, is used after **ask** to introduce a noun clause.	
c) Sara **asked** me **if** I was ready.	**Whether** has the same meaning as <u>if</u>.
(d) Sara **asked** me **whether** I was ready. (e) Sara **asked if** I was ready.	The object pronoun (me) may be ommited after ask.
(f) Sara **wanted to know if** I was ready. (g) Sara **wondered if** I was ready. (h) Sara **inquired whether or not** I was ready.	In addition to **ask**, yes/no questions can be reported by using **want to know, wonder,** and **inquire**.

Unit 2

Exercise 2.2 Oral
(Practice using <u>ask if</u>)

> **Example:** **Student A:** Are you happy?
> **Student B:** (Peter) asked me if I was happy.
> **or:** (Peter) wanted to know if I was happy.

1. Are you hungry?
2. Can you come to my house tonight?
3. Do you have a computer?
4. Did you move to a new town?
5. Do you know how to whistle?
6. Are you going to call me tonight?
7. Can you speak Italian?
8. Do you think it's going to snow?
9. Did you enjoy your trip?
10. Do you know whether or not (........) is single?

- In spoken English as well as in informal written English, sometimes native speakers change noun clause verbs to past forms and sometimes they don't.
- Immediate reporting, **Informal:** (Peter) asked me if I'm happy.
- Reported speech, **Formal sequence of verbs:** (Peter) asked me if I was happy.

Exercise 2.7

Complete the sentences by changing the Quoted Speech to Reported Speech. Practice using the formal sequence of tenses.

> **Example:**
> Brian said, "Do you work?"
> Brian asked me *__if I worked__*.

1. He said, "Do you live around here?"

   He asked me _____.

2. Kathy said to Paul, "Do you want to move in with me?"

   She wanted to know if _____.

3. Chris said to Jenny, "Are you going to go downtown tomorrow?"

   He asked Jenny if _____.

4. I said "Have you ever been to Paris?"

   I inquired whether or not _____.

5. She said to me, "Are we allowed to smoke in here?"

   She wondered if _____.

6. He said, "Can I park here?"

   He inquired whether or not _____.

7. Liz said to Jean, "Did you go to the party?"

   Liz wanted to know if _____.

8. He said, "Can we still get tickets to the concert?"

   He asked if _____.

9. I said, "Is Janet absent today?"

   I inquired whether or not _____.

10. My mother said, "Are you hungry?"

    She wondered if _____.

Grammar Focus

REPORTED SPEECH : WH- QUESTIONS

We can report questions with verbs like **ask, wonder** and **want to know**.
Wh – questions have words like <u>when</u>, <u>what</u>, <u>which</u> or <u>how</u>, both in direct and reported speech.

DIRECT QUESTION	REPORTED QUESTION
"When did you start singing, Lisa?"	Paul asked Lisa when she had started singing.
"What's the time?"	I wondered what time it was.
"Where is the City Hall?"	Someone wanted to know where the City Hall was.
"Where can we go tonight?"	They were asking where they could go tonight.
"How can we learn?"	They wanted to know how they could learn.

Remember: In a reported question, the subject comes before the verb, as in a statement.
- Paul asked Lisa when she started singing.
- ~~Paul asked Lisa when did she start singing.~~

Exercise 2.8

The Tense Change
Listen to Brian telling his friends about a job interview he went to last week.
Fill in the blanks with the correct reported question.

INTERVIEWER: **BRIAN:**

1. Where were you born? — The interviewer asked me <u>where I had been born.</u>
2. How old are you? — She wanted to know _____.
3. Where do you live? — She asked me _____.
4. Where have you worked before? — I remember she wanted to know _____.
5. Why do you want the job? — She asked me _____.
6. Who told you about this opening? — She wondered _____.
7. How much do you hope to earn? — She wanted to know _____.
8. When can you start? — And finally, she asked _____.

Unit 2

Exercise 2.9

Practice reported questions.

A. These people went to a tourist information center yesterday. What did they want to know?

"What are the most interesting sights?"
1.

"Which hotel is the cheapest?"
2.

"How much are the guided tours?"
3.

"What shows are there?"
4.

"Where can I buy city maps?"
5.

"Which museum is the most interesting?"
6.

"How often do the buses run?"
7.

"What time do shops close?"
8.

"What time do banks open on Saturday?"
9.

"Where is the nearest public parking in the area?"
10.

Unit 2

B. Read the questions from A and finish the reported questions.

1. She wanted to know ___*what the most interesting sights were*_____.
2. He wanted to know _____.
3. He wondered _____.
4. She was asking _____.
5. Liz wanted to know _____.
6. Tom wondered _____.
7. She was asking _____.
8. Michael wondered _____.
9. She wanted to know _____.
10. He was asking _____.

Exercise 2.10

Class Activity.

Speaker A: Ask a question on any of the following topics, whatever comes into your mind. Use question words (when, how, where, what, why, etc.).
Speaker B: Answer the question in a complete sentence.
Speaker C: Report what Speaker A and Speaker B said.

Example:	Tomorrow.

Speaker A (Peter): What are you going to do tomorrow?
Speaker B (Mike): I'm going to do my laundry.
Speaker C (You): Peter asked Mike what he was going to do tomorrow, and Mike replied that he was going to do his laundry.

1. Art
2. Culture
3. Music
4. Fashion
5. Tonight
6. This city
7. Vacation
8. Next year
9. English
10. Television
11. Next weekend
12. Sports
13. Weather
14. Book
15. Movie

34 | INTERACTIONS

Unit 2

Guided Conversation

Follow the model conversation and practice. What did he/she say?

Example: (your mother)
"I am coming over to visit."

A: Did I tell you that <u>your mother called yesterday</u>?
B: Really? What did <u>she</u> say?
A: She said <u>she was coming over to visit</u>.

1. (the computer technician)
"The computer is ready. You can pick it up anytime."

2. (my sister)
"I've been sick all week."

3. (Your friend Mike)
"I can't go to the party on Saturday."

4. (Your best friend)
"I want to get you a birthday present, but I'm broke!"

5. (Uncle Charlie)
"I'll send you a postcard from Rome."

6. (my friend from upstairs)
"I've been fired."

7. (the repairman)
"I can't fix the TV by Monday."

8. (grandpa)
"I'll be arriving this Friday at 6:00 p.m."

9. (Your friend Julie)
"I think I'm in love."

10. On your own.

Unit 2

Pronunciation Section

Phonological Feature

> **LINKING WITH -S**
>
> When a final **-s** is followed by a vowel, the sounds are linked. The **-s** sounds like part of the next word.
>
> **Example:** Dr. Smith also work**s** in Saint Michael's hospital.

Exercise 2.11

A. Practice the following sentences.

- Liz uses a computer every day.

- She studies at Morris High School.

- Tina cooks Italian food on weekends.

- Paul looks at her constantly.

- Ann smokes a cigarette after dinner.

B. Listen carefully and complete the sentences with the missing words. Mark the linking sounds.

1. Charles _____ _____ Main Street.
2. Peter _____ _____ the race, too.
3. Mr. Ramos _____ _____ the hospital.
4. He _____ _____ new job in two weeks.
5. Mrs. Robinson _____ _____ different meal every day.

Unit 2

Grammar Focus

PHRASAL VERBS (TWO-WORD and THREE-WORD VERBS)

→ The term phrasal verb* refers to a verb and a preposition, which together have a special meaning.
   For example: **put + off** means **"postpone"**

→ Sometimes a phrasal verb consists of three parts.
   For example: **put + up + with** means **"tolerate"**.

*Phrasal verbs are also called two-word verbs or three-word verbs.

Separable phrasal verbs:	
(a) I <u>handed</u> my homework <u>in</u> yesterday. (b) I <u>handed in</u> my homework yesterday. **INCORRECT:** I handed in it yesterday.	With separable phrasal verbs, a noun may come either between the verb and the preposition or after the preposition, as in (a) and (b).
Nonseparable phrasal verbs:	
(c) I <u>ran into</u> my old English teacher yesterday. (d) I <u>ran into</u> him yesterday. **INCORRECT:** I ran him into yesterday.	With a nonseparable phrasal verb, a noun or pronoun must follow the preposition, as in (c) and (d).

Note: For more Phrasal Verbs see Appendix 2.

Exercise 2.12

Unscramble the words to make sentences.
In some cases, more than one answer is possible.

Example:
on /Put/your/ winter coat
<u>Put on your winter coat.</u>

1. The/have/out/to/I/form/fill _____.
2. changing/about/job/my/I'm/thinking _____.
3. Will/sister/me/pick/after/up/class/my _____.
4. 6:00/usually/at/up/a.m/get/I _____.
5. Out/he/Sunday/on/rarely/goes _____.
6. Out/still/I/to/answer/the/have/figure _____.
7. Over/problem/the/talked/we _____.
8. Leaving/before/should/you/up/room/your/clean _____.
9. Brazil/we/back/just/got/from _____.
10. Look/grandfather/after/you/to/have/your _____.

Unit 2

Exercise 2.13

Particles
Complete the phrasal verbs with particles from the box. You will use some particles more than once.
(Use reference list on phrasal verbs, Appendix 2.)

Up	Out	Back	Down	Off
On	After	Away	Out	Over

	Phrasal verb	Meaning		Phrasal verb	Meaning
1.	write_____	- write on a piece of paper.	7.	pick_____	- select.
2.	try_____	- put clothing to see if it fits.	8.	keep_____	- continue.
3.	get_____	- leave a train/plane/bus.	9.	find_____	- discover information.
4.	look_____	- be careful.	10.	carry_____	- continue.
5.	do_____	- do again.	11.	look_____	- take care of a child.
6.	take_____	- remove clothes.	12.	turn_____	- raise the volume.

Exercise 2.14

Business Situations. Here are some examples of phrasal verbs in business situations.

A. Practice reading these sentences.

- The company that I work for has to <u>cut back</u> because we have spent a lot of money this year. (= spend less)
- My lawyer will <u>draw up</u> a new contract for the house deal. (= write)
- We mustn't <u>fall behind</u> in the race to develop new products. (=be slower than others)
- The two companies were close to an agreement, but it <u>fell through</u>. (=it didn't work)
- My secretary tried to call you yesterday, but she couldn't <u>get through</u>. (=make contact)
- The company has <u>laid off</u> two hundred workers this year. (=temporarily told workers they have no work)
- Why don't you <u>print out</u> the document. (=print)
- Can I <u>call</u> you <u>back</u> in an hour? (=phone again)
- Large companies sometimes <u>take over</u> small ones. (=take control of)
- A good boss always tries to <u>sort out</u> the difficulties. (=ok)

B. **Business Situations. (Pair work)**
Write a small conversation between two business people. Include at least five phrasal verbs from the sentences above.

Unit 2

New Year's Resolutions

Reading

Every time a New Year approaches, we all ask ourselves the very same questions:
- What is this New Year going to bring us?
- How is it going to be different from the past year?
- What can I do to achieve my personal as well as professional goals?
- Will I finally find the person of my dreams?

Ever since I can remember, I have always asked myself these and other questions. I always strongly commit myself to accomplish all the things I have promised to my family and friends.

These are some of my New Year's resolutions for this coming year:

- I told my friends that I wasn't going to work too much and that I would spend more time with them.
- I told my mother that I was going to eat more healthy food and less junk food.
- I said to my doctor: "OK, Dr. Smith, I'll exercise and rest more."

Finally, I said to myself, "It's time for you to start thinking about your future, having your own family and settling down once and for all."

As you can see, there are many things I've decided to do now that the New Year is just around the corner. I'll try my best to accomplish my goals.

Comprehension Questions

A. Answer the questions in the reading.
B. Discuss your answers with your teacher and classmates.

"My New Year's Resolutions"

Unit 2

Writing

Read this person's list of New Year's resolutions. Find and correct mistakes in the use of phrasal verbs. After you've corrected the whole list, write your own.

PERSONAL GOALS:

- Lose weight. (at least 8 pounds).
- Be a better neighbor, and to get them along with me.
- Keep on exercising at least three times a week.
- Give desserts over (especially cheesecake).
- Clean up my garage at least every three months.
- Do not put my bill payments off.
- Finally ask Sara out on a date!
- Go back to college at least as a part time student.
- Give up smoking.

PROFESSIONAL GOALS:

- Call my clients back.
- Hand my assignments in on time.
- Ask for my boss a raise.
- Straighten my office up.
- Call up my customers personally.
- Write a report down, as soon as I get from my business trips back.

UNIT 3

Content
- Will vs. Going to
- Relative Clauses
- Whatever / Whoever / Wherever / Whenever

"Ask Sara. **She'll** teach you"

01. COMMUNICATION **02.** COMPREHENSION **03.** WRITING **04.** GRAMMAR

Unit 3

I'm tired of winter.

Reading

WARM-UP QUESTIONS

Answer and discuss these questions.

1. What's your favorite season?
2. Where are you going to go for your vacation?
3. What are you going to do there?
4. What will your family do?
5. What are your plans for the future?

As spring break is approaching, two friends are talking about their vacation plans.

Betty: I'm tired of winter and I'm tired of this cold weather.

Jack: Just think... In a few weeks it won't be winter anymore.

Betty: Yes. We're going to go outside and play with our friends.

Jack: It will be sunny and we won't have to wear heavy coats anymore.

Betty: I'm really looking forward to this spring.

Jack: Where are you going to go for your vacation?

Betty: I'm going to stay around here. I'm going to spend a lot of time with my family and friends. What about you and your family?

Jack: I'm going to visit my uncle in Canada. My mother will work in the yard and my father is going to paint the house.

Betty: I can't wait for spring to come.

Jack: Neither can I!

Grammar Focus

EXPRESSING FUTURE TIME: BE GOING TO vs. WILL

To express a PREDICTION —either WILL or BE GOING TO is used:

(a) According to the weather channel, it **will** snow on Monday.	(b) According to the weather channel, it **is going to** snow on Monday.
(c) If you're not careful, you **will** cut yourself	(d) If you're not careful, you**'re going to** cut yourself.

When the speaker is making a prediction, either will or going to is possible.
There is no difference in meaning between **(a)** and **(b)** or **(c)** and **(d)**.

To express a PRIOR PLAN —only BE GOING TO is used:

(e) A: Why did you buy plane tickets? B: Because **I'm going to** go on vacation next week.	(f) Mike called me up last night. He is tired of his job, he**'s going to** quit and find a better one.

When the speaker is expressing a prior plan only **be going to** is used.

In **(e)**: Speaker B has made a prior plan. She decided to go on vacation three months ago. She intends to go on vacation next week.

In **(f)**: Mike made the decision in the past and he intends to act on this decision in the future.

To express WILLINGNESS —only WILL is used:

(g) A: The music is too loud! B: I'll turn it down.	(h) I don't know how to cook. Ask Sara. She'll teach you.

In **(g)**: Speaker B is saying: "I'm willing, I'm happy to turn the music down for you."
He's not making a prediction. He had not made a prior plan to turn the music down. Instead he's volunteering to do it.

In **(h)**: The speaker is sure about Sara's willingness to teach him how to cook.

WILL

Also, for a decision made at the moment

What would you like?   { I'll have a beer.
                       { I'll have chicken.

Unit 3

Exercise 3.1

Read the following situations. Write a prediction. Use *Be + Going to* and the correct information from the box.

| - Eat lunch | - Get a ticket | - Rain |
| - Go on vacation | - Buy a plane ticket | - Give the dog a bath |

1. My neighbors are putting some suitcases in the back of their car.
   _____.

2. A man is driving very fast. A police car is chasing him.
   _____.

3. The sky is dark and gloomy.
   _____.

4. My father has a bucket of water, soap and a brush.
   _____.

5. Tim and his wife are talking to a travel agency.
   _____.

6. It's midday and the Robinsons are driving into a Wendy's* parking lot.
   _____.

*__Wendy's:__ Fast food restaurant popular among Americans.

Exercise 3.2

Complete the following sentences expressing willingness.

| Example: | A: I have to drop off my sister. |
| | B: Don't worry. I'll <u>drop her off</u>. |

1. A: Oh, I have to pick up my mother.
   B: But you look so tired. I'll _____.

2. A: I have to write down all these addresses.
   B: But you look so tired. I'll _____.

3. A: I have to take back these videos.
   B: But you're sick. _____.

4. A: I have to send this package.
   B: Don't you move! _____.

5. A: I have to fill out this application.
   B: But you look worn out. _____.

44 | INTERACTIONS

Unit 3

Exercise 3.3

Circle the correct answer:

1. A: It's warm in here!

   B: Okay. (**I'll open, I'm going to open**) the window.

2. A: I'd like something to drink.

   B: Really? (**I'll make, I'm going to make**) some coffee.

3. A: Where are you going?

   B: To the kitchen. (**I'll make, I'm going to make**) some coffee.

4. A: When you see Larry, can you ask him to call me?

   B: Okay. (**I'll ask him, I'm going to ask him**) to call you.

5. A: What would you like to drink, wine or beer?

   B: Hmm... (**I'll have, I'm going to have**) a beer. Thank you.

6. A: What (**are you going to do, will you do**) tomorrow?

   B: (**I'm going to clean up, I'll clean up**) my house.

7. A: Did you mail that letter for me?

   B: Oh, I'm sorry. I completely forgot. (**I'm going to mail it, I'll mail it**) now.

8. A: I've decided to paint my room.

   B: Really? What color (**are you going to paint it, will you paint it**)?

9. A: I have to drop off my mother at the airport.

   B: You look so tired. (**I'm going to drop her off, I'll drop her off**) for you.

10. A: These bags are so heavy.

    B: (**I'll help you carry them, I'm going to help you carry them**).

Exercise 3.4

Complete with *be going to* or *will*:

1. A: Did you write to your uncle?

   B: Oh no! I completely forgot. I _____ write to him right away.

2. A: I need a pen.

   B: Don't worry. I _____ lend you mine.

3. A: What would you like? Chicken or beef?

   B: Hmmm. I _____ have chicken.

Unit 3

4. A: How is Jose doing?

   B: He's doing fine. By the way, he _____ visit me next month.

5. A: I have to drop off my sister.

   B: You look so tired. _____.

6. A: I don't know how to use this camera.

   B: I _____ show you how, but pay attention.

7. A: I decided something yesterday.

   B: What?

   A: I _____ enroll in college next September.

8. A: Tell me, do you have any plans for the weekend?

   B: I sure do. First, I _____ get a haircut.

   Then, I _____ visit my cousin Benny.

9. A: Oh my God! I forgot my money on the table.

   B: Don't worry. I _____ lend you some.

10. A: Your house needs to be painted.

    B: I know, Samuel and I _____ paint it this weekend.

Grammar Focus

RELATIVE CLAUSES

A clause is a part of a sentence. A relative clause tells us which person or thing, (or what kind of person or thing) the speaker means.

(a) The lady **who** lives next door is very friendly. (b) People **who** live in Spain speak Spanish.	In (a): <u>who lives next door</u> tells us which lady. In (b): <u>who live in Spain</u> tells us what kind of people.
(c) Where are the books?-**They** were on the table. (d) Where are the books **that** were on the table?	We use **that** (not who) when we are talking about things in a relative clause. We use **that** instead of **it/they**.
(e) John was wearing a hat **which** was too big for him.	We use **which** or **that** to refer to things. **That** is less formal than which.
(f) That's the author **whose** book I read.	We use **whose** to refer to people's possessions.

46 | INTERACTIONS

Unit 3

*The relative pronouns who(m), that, which, and whose can be the object of a preposition

Example:

He's the manager. + I work for him. =

- He's the manager whom I work for.
- He's the manager who I work for.
- He's the manager that I work for.
- He's the manager I work for.

*Usage note:** In everyday spoken English and in informal writing, we place the preposition at the end of the clause.

In formal English, we put the preposition at the beginning of the clause.

* Mr. Smith is the man she works <u>for</u>.
* Mr. Smith is the man <u>for who(m)</u> she works.

Exercise 3.5

Complete the sentences using WHO-THAT-WHICH-WHOSE-WHOM.

1. Do you know the girl _____ is talking to Samuel?
2. Could you give me the papers _____ are on the table?
3. I want to see the man _____ life I saved.
4. I want you to meet the man _____ saved my life.
5. Everything _____ happened was my fault.
6. This is the girl _____ mother passed away two months ago.
7. You are the man _____ I love.
8. I would like to meet the woman _____ is giving the speech.
9. Who took the money _____ I left on the table?
10. We talked to the boy _____ had the accident last week.

Unit 3

Exercise 3.6

Make questions. Use WHICH-WHO-THAT.

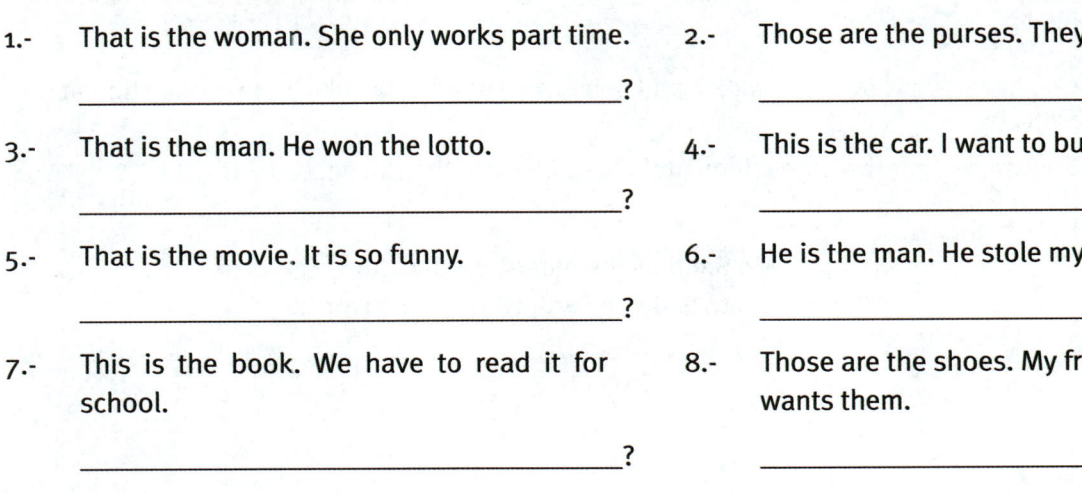

Example:

That is the agent. He lost his job.
<u>Is</u> <u>that</u> <u>the</u> <u>agent</u> <u>who</u> <u>lost</u> <u>his</u> <u>job</u>?

1.- That is the woman. She only works part time.
_____?

2.- Those are the purses. They are on sale.
_____?

3.- That is the man. He won the lotto.
_____?

4.- This is the car. I want to buy it.
_____?

5.- That is the movie. It is so funny.
_____?

6.- He is the man. He stole my mother's car.
_____?

7.- This is the book. We have to read it for school.
_____?

8.- Those are the shoes. My friend Susie wants them.
_____?

Exercise 3.7

Change the sentences using "whose."

Example: I apologized to the woman. I spilled her coffee.
I apologized to the woman **whose** coffee I spilled.

1. The man called the police. His wallet was stolen.

2. I met the woman. Her husband is the president of the corporation.

3. The professor is excellent. I am taking his course.

4. I met a girl. Her hair was red, white and blue.

5. He is the author. I read his books.

6. She is my neighbor. I recently bought her car.

7. They're the Williams. My brother painted their house last week.

8. He is the producer. We watched his films in our class.

9. I excused myself to the man. I stepped on his foot.

Unit 3

Exercise 3.8

Combine the sentences using the relative pronouns Who, Which, That and Whose.

1. The book was good. I read it.
   _____.

2. The teacher liked the composition. I wrote it.
   _____.

3. I saw the woman. She stole the wallet.
   _____.

4. The student is from Mexico. She sits next to me.
   _____.

5. The people are very nice. I visited their house.
   _____.

6. I thanked the man. He helped me.
   _____.

7. I called the man. I hit his car.
   _____.

8. I bought the house. It belonged to Ronald Reagan.
   _____.

9. I like the girl. Her hair is blonde.
   _____
   _____.

10. I apologized to the man. I took his books by mistake.
    _____
    _____.

Unit 3

Exercise 3.9

Error Analysis
Correct the mistakes and rewrite the sentences.

1. He's Mr. Williams. The man that house I painted last summer.
   _____

2. Is that the employee which lost his job?
   _____

3. My friend Charlie has always lived in a house whose belonged to his grandfather.
   _____

4. This is the house who I wanted to buy.
   _____

5. The woman which lives next door is very attractive.
   _____

6. He's the man that my sister works for.
   _____

7. You are exactly the person which I wanted to see.
   _____

8. I apologized to the man that foot I stepped on.
   _____

9. Who took the money who I left on the counter?
   _____

10. He's the actor that movie Steven Spielberg produced.
    _____

11. She is the student whose always late to class.
    _____

12. They are the people who house has been broken into twice this month.
    _____

Unit 3

Guided Conversation

Follow the model and practice with a partner.

Example:

(movie/watch/tonight/The Mummy Returns)

A: What *movie are you going to watch tonight*?
B: I was thinking about *"The Mummy Returns."*
A: Don't you remember? You *watched "The Mummy Returns" just the other night*.
B: You're right! I totally forgot about it.

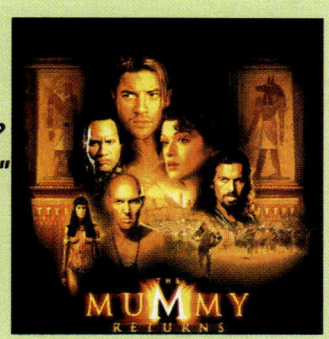

1. (dress/wear/to the party tonight/blue dress)

2. (cook/for dinner tonight/spaghetti)

3. (go dancing with tonight/Sally)

4. (movie/rent tonight/Spiderman)

5. (Night Club/go tonight/"Sunset's Bar and Grill")

6. (eat/with your boyfriend tonight/Chinese food)

7. (drink/ with dinner tonight/red wine)

8. (study/tonight/mathematics)

9. (homework/do tonight/English)

10. (On your own)

Unit 3

Grammar Focus

RELATIVE CLAUSES

We use **that** (or leave it out) when we say **the day/the year/the time**, (etc.) **that something happened:**

Do you remember **the day (that)** you first began to work here?
The last time(that) I saw you, you were very fat.
They haven't been to their country since **the year (that)** the war began.

You can say **the reason why something happens** or **the reason that something happens**. You can also leave out **why** and **that**:

The reason (why/that) I'm upset is because I was not invited to the party.

WHERE You can use **where** in a relative clause to talk about places:

The restaurant – we ate there last night – was very expensive.
The restaurant where we ate last night was very expensive.

Exercise 3.10

Complete the sentences with a relative clause. (the use of *that* is optional)

1. Do you remember the day...... _____.
2. The reason....... _____.
3. Do you know the name of the hotel..... _____.
4. I wasn't in my country the year..... _____.
5. Nineteen sixty-nine was the year .... _____.

Exercise 3.11

Complete the sentences with *Where*..... Use the sentences below to make your relative clauses.

- We spent our vacation there.
- He had bought them there.
- People spend many years there.
- We can eat delicious Mexican food there.
- She was born there.
- You can buy plane tickets there.

Unit 3

1. The place _____ was very beautiful.

2. A prison is a place _____.

3. He took the sneakers back to the store _____.

4. After a long time, she went back to the place _____.

5. A travel agency is a place _____.

6. "La Hacienda" is a restaurant _____.

Pronunciation Section
Reductions

Listen and practice these common reductions for "to":			
want to → wanna		have to → hafta	
need to → needta or needa		has to → hasta	
going to → gonna			

Exercise 3.12

A. Practice these sentences.

1. I want to get a haircut.
   (wanna)

2. She's going to buy a new dress.
   (gonna)

3. He has to pay his bills.
   (hasta)

4. They need to borrow some money.
   (needa)

5. We have to study more.
   (hafta)

B. Complete these sentences.

1. I _____ buy a new car.

2. He _____ pay for my lunch.

3. I'm _____ take a vacation.

4. She _____ borrow some money.

5. I _____ make an important phone call.

Unit 3

Whenever I look back in time...

Reading

WARM-UP QUESTIONS

1. How many jobs have you had in your life?
2. Do you remember the first one?
3. Where did you work?
4. What did you do there?
5. How long did you work there?

Whenever Edward looks back in time, he always remembers the first job he had when he came to Greenville.

His first job was in a car wash. He had to wake up early in the morning. He always returned home exhausted.

Even though his job at the car wash was hard, Edward was happy because he knew that it was a way to help his family have a better future.

After a few months, he was hired as a mechanic at an auto repair shop in a nearby town. Due to Edward's experience as an auto mechanic in his country, he was soon the chief mechanic, and a couple of years later he became the manager of the shop.

Edward has worked since he was very young and his life hasn't been easy, but whenever he looks back in time he feels very proud of himself and he's happy because he knows that his family does, too.

Comprehension Sentences

Write T for true, F for false or M for maybe.

1. Edward lives with his family. _____
2. He was the manager of the car wash. _____
3. He didn't have any experience as a mechanic. _____
4. Edward was very young when he had his first job. _____
5. His family is not proud of Edward. _____

Unit 3

Grammar Focus

-EVER WORDS

Add ever to the words WHAT-WHO-WHERE-WHEN, to form the compounds WHATEVER-WHOEVER-WHEREVER-WHENEVER.

The **ever** adds emphasis to these words and supplies the additional meaning of "regardless of (the situation)" or "no matter what" or "any."

(a) <u>Whoever</u> wins the race, will get a prize of $1,000.	Anyone, no matter who wins the race, will get a prize of $1,000.
(b) <u>Wherever</u> she goes, her dog goes with her.	Regardless of where she goes, her dog goes, too.
(c) <u>Whenever</u> I visit you, I have a good time.	No matter when I visit you, I always have a good time.
(d) <u>Whatever</u> you do, you have to be careful.	No matter what you do, you have to be careful.

Remember:

-Whatever and whoever are considered pronouns.

Whatever: Anything- Everything **Example:** My husband eats whatever I cook
Whoever: Anybody **Example:** Whoever answers this question correctly will get a prize.

-Whenever and Wherever are considered adverbs.

Whenever: Anytime **Example:** You can call me whenever you want.
Wherever: Anywhere/ Everywhere. **Example:** My nephews want to go wherever I go.

Exercise 3.13

Listen to your teacher and circle the correct Adverb or Pronoun.

Example: Mary cries (whenever, wherever) Gary calls her.

1. (Whenever, whoever) took my radio is in big trouble.

2. Robert will have to say (whenever, whatever) we tell him.

3. I will find you (wherever, whenever) you hide.

4. Pedro starts sweating (wherever, whenever) he speaks English.

5. When you are an adult, you can go (whoever, wherever) you want.

6. Lisa says that her husband does (whoever, whatever) she wants.

7. (Whenever, whatever) I go to my country, I stay at my sister's house.

8. If you marry me, I will give you (whatever, whoever) you want.

9. When you finish your homework, you can go (whatever, wherever) you want.

10. It's your party. You can invite (whenever, whoever) you want.

Exercise 3.14

Complete with WHATEVER-WHENEVER-WHEREVER-WHOEVER.

> **Example :** Ann will have to wear <u>whatever</u> I buy.
> After all, I'm her mother.

1. _____ finds my dog will receive a $100 reward.

2. _____ I go to Florida I stay at my uncle's house.

3. You should not buy _____ you see.

4. My niece cries _____ she sees a clown.

5. I take the kids to the movies _____ I can.

6. _____ wrote this letter, is a very romantic person.

7. My chest hurts _____ I breathe.

8. _____ you go _____ you do, I will be right here waiting for you.

9. She has always done _____ she wants.

10. I cry _____ I see my family.

11. _____ you see my wife tell her that I love her.

12. Most teenagers want to do _____ they want.

Unit 3

Home is...

Reading

WARM-UP QUESTIONS

1. How long have you lived in the same house or apartment?
2. How many times have you moved in your life?
3. Do you remember the house you lived in as a child?
4. Could you describe it?
5. Why do people move?

My family and I have lived in the same house for over fifteen years.

Since my father saw the house for the first time and even before he told my mother about it, he had already decided that was the kind of house he wanted us to live in.

We went to the house a couple of times before my father and its owner reached a deal.

Whenever I remember the look on my father's face the day we finally moved in, I get very emotional. It was the kind of look a person has when he has been given the greatest gift of all.

Believe me when I say that it was my father's happiest day ever, and a day I will never forget.

Comprehension Questions

1. How old do you think the speaker is now?
2. Does the speaker remember his childhood with sadness or happiness?
3. Is the speaker a man or a woman? Explain.
4. What's a deal?
5. Which has been your happiest day ever?

The happiest day of my life.

Writing

Finish the story.
Read the following story and then come up with a possible ending.

> Plane transportation is with no doubt one of the fastest and safest ways to go from one place to another.
>
> When I travel, I sometimes encounter unusual situations.
>
> Since I'm a businessman, I have to travel very often. My business trips are always very short and stressful, but not the last one. A few days ago, I was flying between the cities of Orlando and Dallas when suddenly the most unusual thing happened. The cabin crew was about to serve lunch, when the captain announced that due to a serious situation involving a man who was on board, we had to divert our flight to the nearest airport.
>
> Nobody knew what was going on, but some of the passengers started speculating about the possible reasons why our final destination had been abruptly changed. Here is what I heard.

UNIT 4

Content

- Noun Clauses with "If"
- Noun Clauses with a question word
- Directions
- Another One / The Other One
- Others / The Others

> I wonder **whether** Jeff went to the party

01. COMMUNICATION **02. COMPREHENSION** **03. WRITING** **04. GRAMMAR**

Unit 4

We can't fight progress.

Reading

WARM-UP QUESTIONS

Answer and discuss.

1. Do you prefer to live in a big city, or in a rural area? Explain.
2. What are some advantages of living in a populated area?
3. What are some disadvantages?
4. Do you know what urbanistic development is?
5. Are you opposed to urbanistic development? Explain.
6. Do you support it? Explain.

A new shopping center will be built in Greenville. Some neighbors are opposed to this plan and some people support it.

Dave: Have you heard the news?
Jill: No, I haven't. What happened?
Dave: It has recently been announced that a large shopping center will be built in our neighborhood.
Jill: No kidding! Where will they build it?
Dave: Do you know where the old train station is?
Jill: Of course I do. It's right next to Greenville Park.
Dave: Well, that's exactly where the new mall will be.
Jill: I think it's a wonderful idea!
Dave: I'm sorry but I don't agree with you. Can you tell me what the wonderful part is?
Jill: Well, for one thing, that'll make more people visit our town. Besides, it will mean more job opportunities for everybody.
Dave: Yes, but I wonder if you have thought about pollution, more strangers in our neighborhood and higher taxes.
Jill: Maybe you're right, but there's nothing we can do to fight progress.

Comprehension Questions

Answer true or false.

1. Both friends support the idea of the shopping mall.
2. The mall will be built next to the old gas station.
3. Dave thinks building this mall in Greenville isn't a good idea.
4. Jill thinks building the mall is a bad idea.
5. With the new mall, more strangers will come to Greenville.

Unit 4

Grammar Focus

EMBEDDED QUESTIONS or NOUN CLAUSES

When a yes/no question is changed to a noun clause, "if" or "whether" are usually used to introduce the clause.

YES/NO QUESTION	NOUN CLAUSE
Is Lisa at work?	(a) I don't know **if** Lisa is at work.
Does the train stop here?	(b) Do you know **if** the train stops here?
Did Jeff go to the party?	(c) I wonder **whether** Jeff went to the party.

When "if" or "whether" introduce a noun clause, the expression "or not" frequently comes at the end of the clause.

(d) I don't know **if** Lisa is at work **or not**.
(e) I don't know **whether** Lisa is at work.
(f) I don't know **whether** Lisa is at work **or not**.

In (e) : **whether** has the same meaning as **if**.
In (f) : **or not** can come at the end of the noun clause.

Remember:
or not can come immediately after **whether** or at the end of the noun clause, but not right after **if**.

Correct:
I don't know **whether** the train stops here **or not**.
I don't know **whether or not** the train stops here.

I don't know **if** the train stops here.
I don't know **if** the train stops here or not.

Incorrect:
I don't know **if or not** the train stops here.

Exercise 4.1

Complete the sentences by changing the yes/no questions to noun clauses. Introduce the noun clause with *"if"* or *"whether."* Practice the use of *"or not."*

Example: Is Joe at the repair shop? I don't know............
..........**if** Joe is at the repair shop.
..........**if** Joe is at the repair shop or not.
..........**whether** Joe is at the repair shop.
..........**whether** Joe is at the repair shop or not.
..........**whether or not** Joe is at the repair shop.

Unit 4

1. Does Mary live in New York? I don't know..
2. Did Phil go to the party? I don't know...
3. Will the teacher repeat the question? I don't know ....
4. Is your son at home? I don't know ....
5. Was Sara at the restaurant? I wonder ....

Grammar Focus

NOUN CLAUSES THAT BEGIN WITH A QUESTION WORD

The following question words can be used to introduce a noun clause: **When, where, why, how, who, whom, what, which, whose.**

Information questions	Noun clauses
Where does she work?	(a) I don't know where she works.
When did they arrive?	(b) Do you know when they arrived?
What did he say?	(c) Please tell me what he said.
Why is Tina upset?	(d) I wonder why Tina is upset.

Notice:
Question word order is not used in a noun clause.
        INCORRECT: I know where does he work.
        CORRECT: I know where he works.

Exercise 4.2

PAIR WORK - Practice these Noun Clauses beginning with a question word.

1. **A:** Where is the bathroom?
   B: Can you tell me where the bathroom is?

2. **A:** What time is it?
   B: Can you tell me what time it is?

3. **A:** Where is Sandra going?
   B: Could you tell me where Sandra is going?

4. **A:** When did your father come?
   B: Do you remember when your father came?

Unit 4

Exercise 4.3

Complete the sentences by changing the questions to Noun Clauses.
Notice that all the sentences are either Simple Present or Simple Past.

> **Example:** When did David come?
> **Do you know when David came?**

1. How much does this computer cost? Could you please tell me _____.
2. How old is Jane? I don't know _____.
3. Why did Tom leave? I don't know _____.
4. Where does he live? I don't know _____.
5. What time is it? Could you please tell me _____.
6. How far is it to Los Angeles? I wonder _____.
7. Where can I buy a good car? Do you know _____.
8. Where is she? I don't know _____.
9. When does the course end? Can you tell me _____.
10. Why was John absent yesterday? Do you know _____.
11. Where is the bank? Could you please tell me _____.
12. What country is Oshim from? Do you know _____.

Exercise 4.4

Complete the sentences by changing the questions to Noun Clauses.

> **Example:** Who did you see at the library?
> **Tell me who you saw at the library.**

1. Who came to the meeting? Tell me _____.
2. What happened? Tell me _____.
3. Where can I catch the train? Could you please tell me _____?
4. Why is Paul angry? Do you know _____?
5. What time is flight 1709 supposed to arrive? Can you tell me _____?

6. Who is that girl? I wonder _____.

7. Who is in the room? I don't know _____.

8. Whose glasses are those? Could you tell me _____?

9. Whose house is that? I wonder _____.

10. What is a cucumber? Do you know _____?

Exercise 4.5

Change the questions to Noun Clauses.

1. When is your birthday? Can you tell me _____?

2. Is Peter married? Do you know _____?

3. Does Sam work? Do you know _____?

4. Where did Dennis go? Do you remember _____?

5. When was Mary born? Can you remember _____?

6. Whose dog is this? Do you by any chance know _____?

7. Does Gary smoke? Do you know _____?

8. What does Ted sell? Can you tell me _____?

9. Did Lisa take her medicine? Could you please tell me _____?

10. Whose books are these? Do you know _____?

Exercise 4.6

Error analysis: Noun Clauses.
Correct the errors and rewrite the sentences.

> **Example:**
> Please tell me what is your last name.   **Please tell me what your last name is.**

1. I wonder why was Mary late for work. _____.

2. I need to know who is your boyfriend. _____.

3. Be sure to tell the doctor where does it hurt. _____.

4. My son wants to know where do the babies come from. _____.

5. I asked her would she like a cup of coffee or not. _____.

Unit 4

6. No one seems to know when will the baby be born. _____.
7. Do you know where is the teacher from. _____.
8. I wonder does Frank know about the test or not. _____.
9. Please tell me when is flight 620 going to arrive. _____.
10. I've always wondered are they happy with their life. _____.
11. I need to know who are your friends. _____.
12. Please tell me where should I meet you. _____.

Exercise 4.7

Use the words in parentheses to complete the sentences.

1. **A:** Where (Mike go) _____? He's not in his office.

   B: I don't know. Ask the supervisor. He might know where (Mike, go) _____.

2. **A:** I don't know this word. Where (be, my dictionary) _____? Didn't I lend it to you?

   B: I don't have it. Ask Sara where (it, be) _____. I think I saw her using it.

3. **A:** Have you (see, the dog) _____? It was here a minute ago.

   B: I think I saw it in front of Mary's house. Why don't you ask her where (it, be) _____.

4. **A:** When (be, meeting) _____? Is it this week?

   B: I sincerely don't know when (meeting, be) _____. Ask the director.

5. **A:** (be, Mr. Williams) _____ our new English teacher this term?

   B: I don't know. I've also wondered if (Mr. Williams, be) _____ our new English teacher.

Unit 4

Exercise 4.8

Oral Noun Clauses. Answer the following questions. Use "I don't know."

1. Where is the book?
2. Who is that man?
3. What did he buy?
4. What did she do?
5. Where does he live?
6. What is this?
7. Whose pens are these?
8. When is the test?
9. What are the children doing?
10. What is going on?
11. What did they say?
12. Where was Linda born?
13. Who did James see?
14. Whose book is this?
15. When is Janet leaving?
16. Where did Marcos go?

Grammar Focus

ANOTHER ONE – THE OTHER ONE
Another means "one more out of a group of similar items, or one in addition to the one(s) I've already talked about."   **Another** is a combination of *an + other*, written as one word.
The other means "the last one in a specific group, the one that remains from a given number of similar items."
Another and **the other** can be used as an adjective in front of a noun (example, apple) or in front of the word one.

Study these examples:

1. This sandwich is very good. Can I have another one?
2. There were two sandwiches on the table. Jenny ate one and Bob took the other one.
3. John is reading a book this week and he wants to read another one next week.
4. I have two brothers. One is a mechanic and the other one is a teacher.

Unit 4

Exercise 4.9

Complete the sentences with <u>another one</u> - <u>the other one</u>.

1. I have three dogs. Two of my dogs are black and _____ is brown.

2. Rachel has two sisters. One is thin and _____ is fat.

3. I have a pen on the table. I have _____ in my car.

4. Mary has three pens. Two are blue and _____ is red.

5. Mrs. Peterson doesn't like her new car, so she's going to buy _____.

6. Susan has three hats. Two of them are black and _____ is blue.

7. I lent you six dollars. You gave me five dollars back. When are you going to give me _____?

8. This orange juice is so good that I want to drink _____.

9. Kevin has a house in Florida, but he wants to buy _____ in California.

10. This sandwich tastes awful. Could you please make me _____?

11. The city where I live has two shopping malls. One is on Market Street and _____ is on Broadway.

12. I don't like this radio station. Let's listen to _____.

13. Your shirt is dirty. Why don't you put on _____?

14. A: Are you happy with your job?
    B: No. I want to get _____.

15. This movie is boring. Let's watch _____.

Grammar Focus

THE OTHERS - OTHERS	
OTHERS:	Without "the" means "several more out of a group of similar items, several in addition to the ones I've already talked about."
THE OTHERS:	Means "the last ones in an specific group, the remains from a given number of similar items."

Unit 4

Exercise 4.10

Fill in the blanks with ANOTHER ONE, THE OTHER ONE, OTHERS, THE OTHERS.

1. Mary bought three apples. She ate two of the apples. Now she's going to eat _____.

2. Five new people came to my class today. One of them has his books, but _____ don't have theirs.

3. One of the students is studying. I wonder what _____ are doing.

4. Some people work hard. Many _____ don't even have a job.

5. Jenny, I lost the ring you gave me. Can you buy _____ for me?

6. I need to read two books. I read one yesterday, and I'm going to read _____ tomorrow.

7. Life is crazy. Some people are very lucky, while _____ are very unlucky.

8. This CD has ten tracks. Five of them are very good, but _____ are terrible.

9. This soup is cold. Could you bring me _____, please?

10. Look at the employees in this office. Some of them are watching TV, _____ are dancing, and the security guard is sleeping. What a nice office!

Exercise 4.11

Choose the correct answer

1. Ana has two boyfriends. One is a doctor and (another, the other) one is a lawyer.

2. Linda knows a lot of people. Some of them work in offices. (Another, Others) work in hospitals.

3. This book is too boring. Can you lend me (the other, another) one?

4. This orange is delicious. Can you give me (the other, another) one?

5. I have two brothers. One is a teacher and (another, the other) is a lawyer.

6. I have to study three chapters for the test. I studied two yesterday. I'll study (another, the other) one tomorrow.

Unit 4

Guided Conversation

GIVING DIRECTIONS. Give directions by using the following phrases.

walk up	make a right	on the left	behind
walk down	make a left	next to	at the corner of
walk along	on the right	across from	between

Can you help these people get to their destinations? Follow the model and practice with a partner.

Police Station　**Value Supermarket**

Courthouse　**Dry Cleaner**

MAIN Street

County Jail　**Unemployment Office**

Bank　**City Hall**

Example:
(you are at the Police Station and you want to go to the county jail)

A: Excuse me. Can you tell me how to get to the <u>county jail</u> from here?
B: Sure. Just walk <u>down two</u> blocks on Main Street and you'll see it <u>on the right</u>, across from <u>the Unemployment office</u>.
A: Thank you.
B: My pleasure!

1. (from the County Jail to Value Supermarket)

2. (from the Police Station to City Hall)

3. (from the Unemployment Office to the Dry Cleaners)

4. (from the Bank to the Courthouse)

5. (from the Police Station to Value Supermarket)

Unit 4

6. (from the County Jail to City Hall).

7. (from the Bank to the Dry Cleaners)

8. (from the Dry Cleaners to the Courthouse).

Guided Conversation

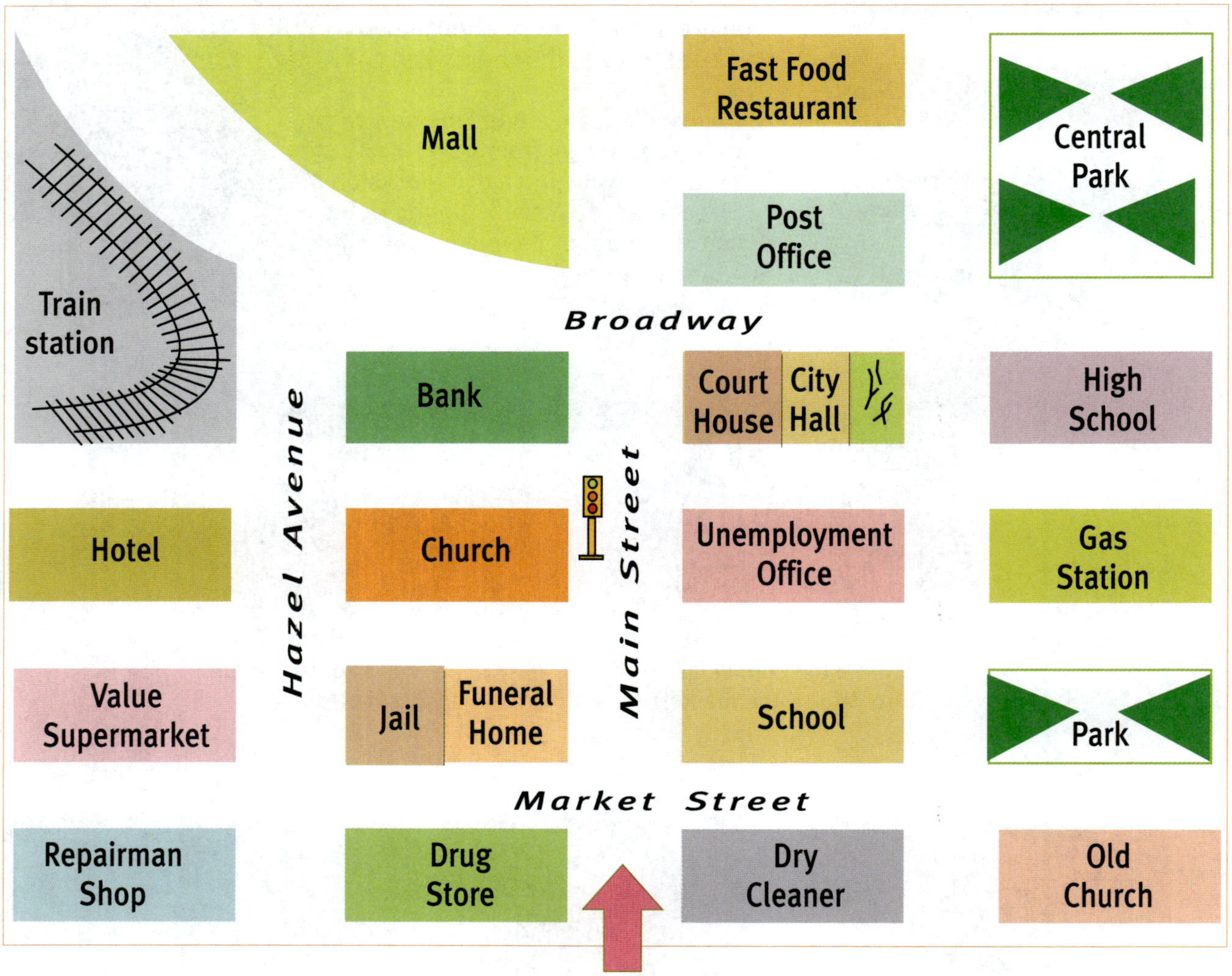

		Fast Food Restaurant	Central Park
Train station	Mall	Post Office	
	Bank	Court House / City Hall 	High School
Hotel	Church	Unemployment Office	Gas Station
Value Supermarket	Jail / Funeral Home	School	Park
Repairman Shop	Drug Store	Dry Cleaner	Old Church

Hazel Avenue runs vertically on the left; *Main Street* runs vertically through the middle. *Broadway* runs horizontally at the top; *Market Street* runs horizontally at the bottom.

Follow the model conversation and practice with a partner.

| Straight | Up | Down | Left | Right. |

70 | INTERACTIONS

Unit 4

1. (City Hall/between the court house and the Chinese restaurant)

Example:

(bank/ in front of the church)
A: Excuse me, but I'm new in town and I think I'm lost. Could you tell me *where the bank is*?
B: Of course, just *walk three blocks up, and then make a left at the light*. You'll see *it in front of the church*. You can't miss it.
A: Thanks for your help.
B: You're welcome and good luck.

2. (Gas station/across from the park)

3. (County jail/next to the funeral home)

4. (Unemployment office/behind the school)

5. (Value supermarket/at the corner of Market St. and Hazel Ave)

6. (Dry cleaner/across from the old church)

7. (Train station/in front of the Mall)

8. (Central Park/behind the high school)

9. (Post office/at the corner of Broadway and Main street)

10. (On your own)

Unit 4

Pronunciation Section

Phonological Feature

> **LINKING SOUNDS ("one of the" + adjective)**
>
> In **one of the,** the words are linked. We usually don't hear the "f" in "of."
>
> Soccer is one of the most popular sports in the world.

Exercise 4.12

A. Practice these sentences.

1. China was one of the first countries to use paper money.
2. Brazil is one of the few Latin American countries where emeralds are mined.
3. Madonna is one of the most controversial singers ever.
4. Cellular phones have been one of the most popular inventions of the 20th Century.
5. My father is one of the best chess players I know.

B. Complete these sentences with *One of the* and the adjective that you hear.

1. The white elephant is _____ ___ _____ _____ animals on earth.
2. Discovery channel is _____ ___ _____ _____ _____ channels on TV.
3. Karla was _____ ___ _____ _____ _____ girls in my class last term.
4. Kublai Khan was _____ ___ _____ _____ emperors of China.
5. January is _____ _____ _____ _____ months of the year.

Unit 4

Things that Matter

Reading

Whenever you think about the future, what changes do you think this new century will bring? Consider for instance:

- Education
- Medical advances
- Technological advances
- Internet
- Lifestyle (housing, food, etc.)

What do you think your life will be like 10 or 20 years from now? Will it be the same? Will it be different?

Many people think, for example, that education will play a very important role in modern society. Education will definitely be the key to future success.

In an era of contrasts between satellite communication and designer clothes, when everybody is looking for both luxury and technology, our lives change with every minute that passes. However, we should remember that there are some things that will always be the same: family, values and friendship. These things are the ones that really count and make the world a beautiful place to live in.

Comprehension Questions

1. Answer the questions from the reading.
2. Do you agree with the reading? Why? Why not?
3. Think about 3 possible medical advances that could happen in the near future.
4. Think about 3 possible technological ones.
5. What do you think houses will be like?

Writing

For writing and discussion.

It's the year 2025. Due to dramatic weather changes on the planet, living conditions on earth are very different than a hundred years ago.

Besides the possible technological advances, how do you think life will be like in the year 2025?
Consider: Housing, food, education, jobs, medical advances, etc.

UNIT 5

Content
- Adjectives and Adverbs
- Adverbs of Manner
- Adverbs of Frequency

"He'll rent his apartment **quickly**"

01. COMMUNICATION **02. COMPREHENSION** **03. WRITING** **04. GRAMMAR**

Unit 5

I'll never dance gracefully.

Reading

Peter's wife is very discouraged because they've been married for over two years, and he had promised her that he would learn how to dance. Peter's wife dances gracefully. In fact, she won two dancing contests when she was younger. Listen to their conversation.

Peter: I have told you a thousand times; I'll never learn how to dance.
Rita: But, honey, you promised that you were going to learn how to!
Peter: I know, I know. It's just that I dance so badly that I'm afraid people will laugh at me if I do.
Rita: I totally agree with you. People can be so mean sometimes. Just remember that I love you and that I'll never laugh at you, not even if you dance terribly.
Peter: Thanks dear, I love you too but....
Rita: I have an excellent idea!
Peter: Really? What is it?
Rita: I know this famous dance academy in town. Maybe you could take some dance lessons with them. I'm sure you'll learn very quickly.
Peter: Don't be so sure. However, since I know this is important for you, I'll do it.
Rita: Wonderful! I'm definitely sure you'll become a graceful dancer in no time.

Comprehension Questions

A. Answer the following questions:

1. Do you like to dance?
2. Are you a good dancer?
3. Have you ever taken dance lessons?
4. What's your favorite kind of music when it comes to dancing?

B. Answer True or False:

1. The word "over" in the first line of the paragraph means "more than." _____
2. Peter's wife doesn't dance gracefully. _____
3. The word "mean" stands for "not nice." _____
4. They've been married for over 5 years. _____

Unit 5

Grammar Focus

ADJECTIVES AND ADVERBS

ADJECTIVES

(a) Martha is a **beautiful woman**.
         (adj)   (noun)
(b) The **young man** opened the door.
         (adj) (noun)
(c) I need to buy a **brown jacket**.
                    (adj)   (noun)
	Adjectives describe nouns. In grammar we say that adjectives **"modify"** nouns. The word **"modify"** means **"change a little."**
	
	Example: **beautiful** woman
	                  intelligent woman
	                  ugly woman
	                  good woman

(d) I like to sing **old songs**. **Incorrect:** olds songs.	**An adjective is neither singular nor plural.** A final –s is never added to an adjective.

ADVERBS OF MANNER

(a) She speaks **softly**.
                (adverb)
 	
(b) He opened his present **rapidly**.
                                      (adverb)
 	
c) Richard dances **gracefully**.
                          (adverb)
	Adverbs modify verbs. Often they answer the question **"How?"**
	   In (a) How does she speak?
	         Answer: **quickly**.
	Adverbs are often formed by adding –ly to an adjective:
	         Adjective: **Soft**
	         Adverb: **Softly**

> **Be careful!**
>
> Do not put an adverb of manner between the verb and the direct object.
>   **Example:** He'll rent his apartment quickly.
>   Not ~~He'll rent quickly his apartment.~~

UNIT 5 | 77

Unit 5

SPELLING RULES TO FORM ADVERBS FROM ADJECTIVES

Adverbs of manner are often formed by adding –ly to adjectives.

slow – slow**ly**	quick - quick**ly**	clear – clear**ly**
bad – bad**ly**	loud – loud**ly**	soft – soft**ly**
beautiful – beautifu**lly**	quiet – quiet**ly**	extreme - extreme**ly**

Exceptions: fast – fast   early – early
  hard – hard   good – well

We use adverbs when:

You are describing or giving more information about action verbs.
 Example: She **described** the suspect **perfectly**. (manner)

Describing or giving more information about adjectives or other adverbs.
 Example: She's **absolutely beautiful**.
 Example The salesman will sell the car **very quickly**.

*Some adverbs of manner have **two forms** : one with -ly and one without -ly.
  slowly or **slow**   **loudly** or **loud**
  quickly or **quick**   **clearly** or **clear**

(A) Don't walk so **quickly**; I can't keep up the pace.
  Don't walk so **quick**; I can't keep up the pace.

(B) Speak **slowly**, I can't understand a word you're saying.
  Speak **slow,** I can't understand a word you're saying.

▲
Exercise 5.1

A. Write the adjectives or adverbs:

ADJECTIVES	ADVERBS
1. Careful	
2.	Accurately

ADJECTIVES	ADVERBS
3. Easy	
4. Wonderful	

Cont....

ADJECTIVES	ADVERBS
5.	Frequently
6. Quiet	
7.	Well
8. Nice	

ADJECTIVES	ADVERBS
9. Unfortunate	
10.	Heavily
11. Slight	
12. Sudden	

Exercise 5.2

Choose the correct adverb or adjective:

1. Please come (**quick, quickly**).

2. Jennifer left (**sudden, suddenly**).

3. Robert opened the door (**quiet, quietly**).

4. This area is so (**nice, nicely**).

5. The house is (**nice, nicely**).

6. Mary writes poems (**beautiful, beautifully**).

7. Mary's poems are (**beautiful, beautifully**).

8. This is a (**good, well**) house.

9. This sandwich is so (**good, well**).

10. His (**sudden, suddenly**) disappearance surprised us.

11. The teacher's explanation is always (**clear, clearly**).

12. I heard a (**loud, loudly**) noise.

13. That car is very (**slow, slowly**).

14. The new man did the work (**rapid, rapidly**).

15. My test was very (**easy, easily**).

16. I saw a very (**nice, nicely**) movie last week.

17. My mother sings very (**good, well**).

18. Vincent is a very (**good, well**) man.

19. You speak very (**nice, nicely**).

20. Dennis is very (**quiet, quietly**).

21. Anna was very (**beautiful, beautifully**).

22. Rosa draws very (**sloppy, sloppily**).

23. I can't believe James dances so (**good, well**).

24. Hector explains mathematics very (**bad, badly**).

25. Julia is a (**quickly, quick**) runner.

Unit 5

Exercise 5.3

Choose the correct adverb to complete the sentences:

patiently	intentionally	seriously	unexpectedly
badly	perfectly	temporarily	easily
suddenly	heavily	accurately	suspiciously

1. James and Peter had to wait for a long time and didn't complain. They just waited _____.

2. My brother was _____ injured in a car accident last week.

3. I don't think she liked me. She looked at me so _____.

4. I just got a job in a supermarket, but I won't stay there for long. I'm only working there _____ _____ until I can find a better job.

5. Mrs. Olmen is an excellent typist. She types very _____.

6. We took John to the hospital because he was bleeding _____.

7. We didn't know that Aunt Rita was coming. She arrived so _____.

8. I'm going to study English until I speak _____.

9. I didn't mean to hit you. I didn't do it _____.

10. Jane didn't want to go out because It was raining _____.

11. We didn't have any difficulty winning the soccer match. We won _____.

12. The fire started _____. They didn't notice it until it was too late.

Unit 5

Guided Conversation

Follow the model.

A reckless teenager

A. In my opinion, she's a reckless teenager.
B. I think so, too. She acts very recklessly.

1. A wonderful teacher

2. An eloquent speaker

3. A slow secretary

4. Incredible dancers

5. A nice painter

6. A graceful singer

7. A dishonest player

8. An incredible writer

9. (On your own)

Unit 5

Grammar Focus

ADJECTIVES AND ADVERBS

We also use adverbs before adjectives and other adverbs.

Incredibly fast   (adverb + adjective)
Extremely nice   (adverb + adjective)
Surprisingly clearly   (adverb + adverb)

I love that restaurant; the service is **incredibly fast**.
Treat her with respect; she's **extremely nice**.
The student explained the problem **surprisingly clearly**.

You can use an adverb before a past participle.

The party was **perfectly organized**.
The little boy was **seriously injured** in the fire.
I was **totally surprised** to hear the news.

Exercise 5.4

Choose two words (an adverb and adjective) to complete each sentence:

ADVERBS			ADJECTIVES		
Carefully	Seriously	Absolutely	Cheap	Sorry	Enormous
Completely	Unusually	Fully	Changed	Insured	Quiet
Extremely	Reasonably	Slightly	Damaged	Planned	Ill

1. I'm _____ _____ about breaking the window.

2. I went back to my hometown after 15 years and everything had _____ _____.

3. My sister is normally very talkative, but she has been _____ _____ lately.

4. It wasn't a serious fire, the house was _____ _____ _____.

5. I thought this car was really expensive, but it was _____ _____.

6. Janet's grandmother is _____ _____ in the hospital.

7. My car was completely destroyed in the accident, luckily it was _____ _____.

8. What a big house! It's _____ _____.

9. Patty's wedding was perfect because it was _____ _____.

Unit 5

Exercise 5.5

Directions: Underline and label the Adjectives (ADJ) and Adverbs (ADV) in the sentences.

Example :
An <u>unusually</u> <u>big</u> dog chased me while I was jogging in the park.
    (adverb) (adj)

1. A terrible storm suddenly hit the small town.

2. Mike carefully told his old mother the bad news.

3. A young girl gently told me to follow her.

4. The best player on the team was always late for practice.

5. The careless child hit the poor cat with a long stick.

6. On busy Fridays, I usually work until 6:00p.m and occasionally until 8:00 p.m.

7. Has your mother already quit smoking?

8. I always stay home on cold winter nights.

9. An unusually large number of people went to the meeting.

10. Fred asked me an easy question. I answered it quickly.

11. My neighbors had a big fight just the other night.

12. The little boy was seriously injured in the terrible car accident.

13. I'm so sorry, but I forgot to tell you about the party.

14. She's extremely careful with her money. Some people say she's stingy.

15. I carefully finished the difficult test.

Unit 5

Grammar Focus

ADJECTIVES AND ADVERBS	
GOOD/WELL	
Good is an adjective: They are very good children.	The adverb is **well**: They are well behaved.
We often use well with past participles (behaved, dressed, mannered, etc) Well behaved (not <u>good behaved</u>) Well dressed (not <u>good dressed</u>), etc.	
Exception: **Well** is also an adjective with the meaning "in good health"	
"How are you today?"	"I'm very well, thank you." (correct) "I'm very good, thank you." (incorrect)
FAST/HARD/LATE	
These words are both adjectives and adverbs:	
Adjective	**Adverb**
Liz is a very fast typist. Peter is a hard worker. The bus was late.	Liz can type very fast. Peter works hard (not <u>works hardly</u>) I woke up late this morning.
Lately is an adverb. It means "recently". - Have you seen any good movie lately?	
HARDLY Hardly has a completely different meaning from hard:	
Hardly = almost not	Example: "I can't kiss you", she said, "We hardly know each other."
We often use hardly with can/could:	Example: -Speak louder, I can hardly hear you. - My back hurt all night, I could hardly sleep.
We use hardly with <u>any</u>/<u>anyone</u>/ <u>anything</u>/<u>anywhere</u>:	Example: -"How much money do you have?" "Hardly any." (= almost none) - The meeting was a failure. Hardly anyone attended. (= almost no one) - I think my dog is sick. It hardly ate anything. (= almost nothing) - She prefers to stay home. She hardly goes anywhere. (= almost nowhere)
Hardly ever = almost never:	Example: My sister hardly ever goes out on the weekends. My sister almost never goes out on the weekends.

Unit 5

Exercise 5.6

Write Right or Wrong.   Right   Wrong

1. I hope your parents are good.   _____   _____
2. Please! Don't walk so fast.   _____   _____
3. Today is Friday. Let's not work so hard.   _____   _____
4. My mother is back from the hospital. She's good now.   _____   _____
5. I tried hardly to remember her address, but I couldn't.   _____   _____
6. The apartment looks nicer and very comfortable.   _____   _____
7. It was a hard decision, but somebody had to make it.   _____   _____
8. Why don't you come for a visit? It would be wonderful to see you.   _____   _____
9. My landlord is happy married.   _____   _____
10. I heard about your new roommate. Is he a good person?   _____   _____

Exercise 5.7

Finish the sentence with "well" + one of the following words.

| dressed | kept | described | mannered | done | ventilated | planned |

1. Thank you for a job well _____.
2. Whenever you go to a job interview, you have to be well _____.
3. The suspect was so well _____ that he was caught in less than two days.
4. Her kids are so well _____ that she never has any problem with them.
5. Laura's age is a well_____ secret.
6. I really enjoyed the book. The characters were well _____.
7. The existence of aliens is a secret well _____.
8. There's nothing better to impress your date, than to be well _____.
9. If you want your party to be a complete success, it has to be well _____.
10. According to modern architecture a room should be well _____.

Exercise 5.8

Make sentences with "Hardly." Use the words in parentheses (...).

1. You look different. (recognized)   I _____.
2. When she found out the news (could/speak) she _____.

Unit 5

3. I don't feel like working today. (slept/last night) I _____.
4. Turn up the volume. (can/hear) I _____ the music.
5. Your handwriting is so small. (can/read) I _____.
6. She was so scared. She could (talk) _____.
7. I was so tired yesterday. I could (walk) _____.
8. I want to go on vacation. I can (wait) _____ for school to finish.
9. Mary wanted to tell her husband about his surprise party. She could (keep) _____ the secret.
10. That tree is blocking the view. I can (see) _____ the house from here.

Exercise 5.9

Complete the sentences with hardly + any/anyone/anything/anywhere/ever.

1. I love going out, but I _____ go out at night.
2. She's not very friendly. _____ likes her.
3. Last winter wasn't very cold. There was _____ snow.
4. We used to be next door neighbors, but now we _____ see each other.
5. I hate this town. There's _____ to do and _____ to go.
6. I'm new in town. I _____ know _____.
7. She's so shy, she _____ speaks in class.
8. The girl was so injured after the accident, she could _____ say _____ to the police.

Grammar Focus

FREQUENCY ADVERBS						
ALWAYS	USUALLY	OFTEN	SOMETIMES	SELDOM	RARELY	NEVER
100%	99% - 90%	90% - 75%	75% - 25%	25% - 10%	10% - 1%	0%

Always, usually, often, sometimes, seldom, rarely and **never** are called "frequency adverbs."
They come between the subject and the simple present verb.*

SUBJECT	+	FREQUENCY ADVERB	+	SIMPLE PRESENT VERB

Unit 5

FREQUENCY ADVERBS

Subject + { always, usually, often, sometimes, seldom, rarely, never } + Verb	(a) Peter **always** wakes up at 7:00 a.m.
	(b) Liz **usually** wakes up at 7:00 a.m.
	(c) They **often** go to the movies.
	(d) I **sometimes** watch TV at night.
	(e) We **seldom** go to church.
	(f) Mary **rarely** eats breakfast.
	(g) Bob **never** drinks alcohol.

*Some Frequency Adverbs can also come at the beginning or at the end of a sentence. for example:
Sometimes I eat lunch at 2:00 p.m.   I eat lunch at 2:00 p.m. **sometimes**.

Exercise 5.10 Oral

Place the Frequency Adverb into these sentences.

always	.... 1. I <u>always</u> drink water.
usually	.... 2. I go to bed at midnight.
often	.... 3. I drink a glass of milk before going to bed.
never	.... 4. I eat between meals.
seldom	.... 5. I take a shower on Sunday.
sometimes	.... 6. I have a beer with my lunch.
rarely	.... 7. I go to the doctor.
never	.... 8. I lie.
always	.... 9. I get to work on time.
usually	.... 10. I go to the movies on Saturday evenings.
rarely	.... 11. I go out in winter.
never	.... 12. I travel by plane on Friday the 13th.

Exercise 5.11

Write about your daily activities. (use the Frequency Adverbs and the following cues).

1. wake up
2. eat breakfast at 6:00 in the morning
3. take a shower
4. put on my clothes
5. go to work at 8:30 a.m.
6. listen to music on my way to work
7. come back home around 6:00 p.m.
8. go to the movies
9. talk on the phone
10. speak English with my friends
11. go to bed after midnight
12. dream about my country
13. read a newspaper
14. write to my family
15. go dancing
16. drink alcohol
17. cut my hair
18. spend time with my friends
19. drink milk
20. kiss my wife/husband/boyfriend/girlfriend/etc.

Unit 5

Grammar Focus

USING FREQUENCY ADVERBS WITH BE
SUBJECT + BE + FREQUENCY ADVERB + PREDICATE
Mike + is + { always, usually, often, sometimes, seldom, rarely, never } + late for work.

Exercise 5.12

Add the Frequency Adverb in italics to the sentence.

1. *always* — Peter is on time for dinner.

2. *never* — Gloria is absent from class.

3. *usually* — My father eats breakfast in bed on Sunday.

4. *rarely* — Sheila cooks her own food.

5. *sometimes* — I am late for appointments.

6. *usually* — I study one day before taking a test.

88 | INTERACTIONS

Unit 5

| 7. *always* | Mary is thinking about her boyfriend. |

___

| 8. *sometimes* | The Robinson family goes to the beach on weekends. |

___

| 9. *never* | My boss is satisfied with my work. |

___

| 10. *seldom* | She drinks tea. |

___

Exercise 5.13

Respond in complete sentences.

> **Example:**
> **What is something that** you always do on Sunday morning?
> **Response:** I always sleep late on Sunday morning.

What is something that.....

.....you never do?

.....you almost always do before you go to bed?

.....a lazy person rarely does?

.....people in your country always or usually do to celebrate Christmas?

.....you usually do?

.....you just did?

.....you sometimes do before you come to class?

.....you rarely do?

.....you have already done?

.....a rude person usually does?

.....reckless drivers never do?

.....your roommate/spouse often does?

Unit 5

Exercise 5.14

Adverbs and Adjectives: Susan wrote a letter to a friend. Complete the letter. Use the correct form of the words in parentheses ( ).

Dear Martha,

I'm _____ 1.(total) exhausted! Dan and I finished moving into our new apartment today. It was a lot of _____ 2. (hard) work, but everything worked out _____.3. (good).

The apartment looks _____ 4. (nice). It's _____ _____ 5.(extreme) 6.(comfortable). The only problem is with the heat. I always feel _____. 7. (cold). We'll have to speak to the landlord about it. He seems _____ _____ 8.(pretty) 9.(friendly) .People tell me that the neighborhood is very_____.10.(safe) .That's _____ 11.(real) 12.(important), because I get home _____ 13.(late) from work. I hate it when the streets are _____ _____ 14.(complete) 15.(empty) as they were in our old neighborhood. Shopping is _____ 16.(good), too. We can get to all the stores very_____ _____17. (easy) .The bus stop is _____ 18.(near) the apartment,and the buses run_____.19.(frequent)

Why don't you come for a visit? It would be _____ 20. (wonderful) to see you. I haven't seen you since our wedding.

Please write.
Love,
Susan

Exercise 5.15

Error Analysis.
Find the mistake(s) and rewrite these sentences.

1. The song was nice interpreted by the beautifully singer.
   _____.

2. Our neighbors are extremely usually quiet.
   _____.

3. A: How's the new secretary doing?
   B: Very good. Although she's slightly quietly, and a badly typist.
   _____.

4. I'm fully responsible for my actions always.
   _____.

5. My sister seldom is friendly to strangers.
   _____.

6. He came unexpected and left sudden.
   _____.

7. Ann used to be very beautifully.
   _____.

8. I slow understood what she was trying to tell me, but it took me a while to.
   _____.

9. Even though she ran fastly, she didn't win the race.
   _____.

10. I general wake up at 7:00 o'clock every morning, but never I have breakfast.
    _____.

11. Even though Joan dreams always about her country, she's happily living here.
    _____.

12. Be carefully! The soup is extremely hot.
    _____.

Unit 5

Pronunciation Section

Language Discrimination

NEGATIVE CONTRACTION

In a negative contraction, we often do not hear the final "t."

Were ⟶ weren't   is ⟶ isn't

Was ⟶ wasn't   did ⟶ didn't

Could ⟶ couldn't

Exercise 5.16

A. Practice the following sentences.

1. They weren't happy with their gifts.
2. People didn't panic when they saw the accident.
3. The teacher wasn't happy with the exam results.
4. I couldn't be happier.
5. She isn't sure what to do.

B. Complete the sentences with the negative contractions that you hear.

1. The car _____ working.
2. She _____ studying here anymore.
3. We _____ go to the party because I got sick.
4. My parents _____ happy with my grades.
5. Some workers _____ return to work.

Unit 5

An Important Mission

Reading

WARM-UP QUESTIONS

1. Do you watch the news on T.V.?
2. Which are your favorite news broadcasts?
3. Who is your favorite reporter? Why?
4. Do you think it is dangerous to be a reporter? Explain.

Charles Reynolds and Susan Abbot are two well-known reporters from Channel 4 News at 5.

Their job is to look for and cover important and interesting news, as well as interview famous and controversial people worldwide. Some of the people they interview are presidents, ambassadors, movie stars, singers and outlaws.

Their family and friends constantly tell them to be careful and to try not to expose themselves to unnecessary risks, since their job is a very dangerous one.

They have been working as reporters for over ten years now and they know that whatever happens, they can only count on each other.

Just a couple of months ago, their boss assigned them a mission in which they had to fly overseas and cover an armed conflict between two countries.

When they got there, after just a couple of hours in the country, they were confronted with the cruel reality of living in war.

After two weeks of broadcasting live from the conflict zone, they returned to their country and back to their families and daily routine. Now wherever they go, whatever they do or whoever they interview, their trip into a war zone is something they'll never forget.

Comprehension Sentences

Answer T for true, F for false or M for maybe.
1. Being a reporter could be dangerous.
2. Charles and Susan are not famous reporters.
3. Outlaw is a synonym of bandit.
4. Charles's family was confronted with the cruel reality of living in war.
5. They will soon forget their trip into the war zone.

News Broadcaster

Exercise 5.17

Read this newspaper ad which a real estate office posted in a local newspaper. Underline the adjectives and circle the adverbs. Then draw an arrow → from the adjective or adverb to the word it is describing.

WELCOME TO GREENVILLE

Are you looking for a nice place to live?

If the answer is yes, we at Greenville Realtors have the perfect house or apartment for you.

Come and see us at 240 Highland Street, Suite 407.

We have beautiful homes and large apartments for rent in quiet and safe neighborhoods.

You will quickly fall in love with your new home once you see it.

Most of our units are located in beautifully restored buildings, conveniently located within walking distance from wonderful shopping malls, clear ponds and peaceful parks. Rents are affordable.

Writing

Read the newspaper classified ad on apartments and houses for rent.
Write your own classified in which you'll be renting or selling a house.
Make sure you include detailed information such as: location, description, rent, etc. (don't forget to use adjectives and adverbs).

_____
_____
_____
_____
_____
_____
_____
_____
_____
_____
_____
_____

94 | INTERACTIONS

UNIT 6

Content
- Comparative Adjectives
- Short Answers with Infinitives
- Adjectives Followed by Infinitives

"I'm *younger* than you"

01. COMMUNICATION   **02. COMPREHENSION**   **03. WRITING**   **04. GRAMMAR**

Unit 6

Shopping for Bargains

Reading

When it comes to shopping, my friend Becky is an expert. She is the kind of person you can always count on whenever you need to go shopping for bargains.

Just the other day I was in a big dilemma. I had to buy a present for my boss and his wife for their wedding anniversary and I had so little money that I just didn't know what to do.

It was then, when I remembered my friend Becky and I decided to give her an emergency call. This was our conversation:

Janet: Help!! I need your help!
Becky: Is that you Janet?
Janet: Yes, It's me Becky. You've got to help me. Please!
Becky: What's the matter?
Janet: You see, today's my boss's wedding anniversary. I have to get him a present and I have very little money. What can I do?
Becky: Calm down. Let's see ... What could you buy?
Janet: How about a crystal vase? Or a framed picture?
Becky: A crystal vase would be prettier than a framed picture, but....
Janet: I know. It would be more expensive, too!
Becky: Right... I got it! I know this woman who owns an antique store. We could go today and get something prettier and cheaper than a crystal vase or a framed picture.
Janet: That sounds good to me! I'll pick you up at 2:00. Is that OK with you?
Becky: 3:00 is a better time for me.
Janet: OK, see you then.

Comprehension Questions

1. In line #2, what do "bargains" stand for?
2. Where can you shop for bargains in your city?
3. Whose wedding anniversary is it?
4. Are you single or married? If married, when is your wedding anniversary?
5. What do you think Janet should buy for her boss?

Bargains = Low prices

Unit 6

Grammar Focus

COMPARATIVE ADJECTIVES

Comparative adjectives are used to make comparisons between two people or things.

My brother is taller than my sister.
I'm younger than you.
My girlfriend is more beautiful than Mary.
Mathematics is more difficult than Science.

SPELLING RULES

One syllable adjectives add "er".

young ....younger
clean.........................cleaner
cheap.........................cheaper

One syllable adjectives that end in a vowel and a consonant, double the consonant and add "er".

big............................bigger
hot ....hotter
thin...........................thinner

Two or more syllable adjectives use "more".

important....................**more** important
complicated.................**more** complicated
beautiful......................**more** beautiful

Two syllable adjectives that end in "y" change to "i" and add "er".

easy..........................easier (**not** more easy)
happy........................happier (**not** more happy)
funny.........................funnier (**not** more funny)

EXCEPTIONS: good....................better
bad.......................worse
far.........................farther / further

Unit 6

Exercise 6.1

Write the comparative forms for the following adjectives.

1. Big_____
2. Cheap_____
3. Comfortable_____
4. Cold_____
5. Hot_____
6. Large_____
7. Intelligent_____
8. Lazy_____
9. Heavy_____
10. Expensive_____
11. Good_____
12. Important_____
13. Far_____
14. Bad_____
15. Funny_____
16. Wide_____
17. Dangerous_____
18. Safe_____

Exercise 6.2

Complete the sentences. Use the comparative form of the word in parenthesis.

1. The Sunlight Hotel is _____ than The Grand Hotel. (cheap)
2. Math is _____ than English. (difficult)
3. Your apartment is _____ than mine. (large)
4. My roommate is _____ than I am. (lazy)
5. This city is _____ than my city. (clean)
6. My brother is _____ than I am. (tall)
7. In my opinion, Frank is _____ than John. (talented)
8. The Nile River is _____ than the Mississippi river. (long)
9. My English class is _____ than my History class. (interesting)
10. In my opinion, "Clear Cream" leaves your skin _____ than "Nove Cream." (soft)
11. Smith Street is _____ than Main street. (safe)
12. I like my new neighborhood, everything is _____ than in our old neighborhood. (convenient)
13. King Supermarket seems to have _____ prices than A & S Supermarket. (low)

98 INTERACTIONS

Unit 6

Exercise 6.3

Error analysis.
All of the following sentences contain errors.
Find and correct the mistakes.

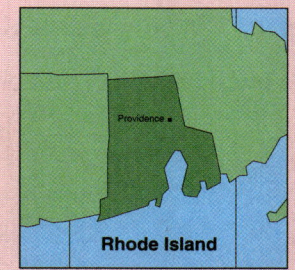
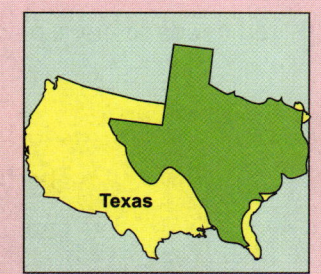

Example:

Texas is large than Rhode Island.
Texas is larger than Rhode Island.

1. Old jeans are usually comfortabler than new ones.
   _____.

2. Mr. Smith teaches gooder than Mr. Williams.
   _____.

3. I like Chinese food more better than Italian food.
   _____.

4. I have one sister and one brother. My sister is more younger than my brother.
   _____.

5. My school is bigger than your school.
   _____.

6. Cats are usually more small than dogs.
   _____.

7. Jack isn't a very good typist. I can type much fast than him.
   _____.

8. Taking a train is much cheap than taking an airplane.
   _____.

9. For some people, learning a second language is more easy than learning chemistry.
   _____.

10. A piano is more heavy than a saxophone.
    _____.

Exercise 6.4 Oral

Fred needs to buy a new car. He can't decide between a blue Ford Explorer and a red Hyundai Elantra.

Which car is nicer, the blue Ford or the red Hyundai?

The blue Ford:	The red Hyundai:
Cap: 6 passengers	**Cap:** 5 passengers
Cost: $22,000.	**Cost:** $15,000
Model: Explorer	**Model:** Elantra
Year: 2002	**Year:** 2000

Write sentences to help Fred decide which car is more convenient for him.

1. _____:_____.
2. _____.
3. _____.
4. _____.
5. _____.

Unit 6

Guided Conversation

Follow the model.

A: I'm confused.
B: What's the matter?
A: Should **I wear the blue suit or the black one to Jane's wedding**?
B: I think you should wear the blue one.
  It's nicer than the black one.

1. buy a bike or a motorcycle. (expensive)

2. go out with Janet or Jill. (pretty)

3. study English or French. (necessary)

4. go on vacation to Florida or Texas. (interesting)

5. buy a stereo or a boom box. (good)

6. take piano or guitar lessons. (easy)

7. buy a new car or an old one. (reliable)

8. cut my hair at Sammy's or Melba's. (experience)

9. (On your own)

Unit 6

Exercise 6.5

Speak up!
Your Opinion Counts!
Compare two restaurants in your city.

Example: In my opinion, Lan's restaurant has more delicious food than John's restaurant

1. Compare two supermarkets around your area.
2. Compare two famous singers.
3. Compare two popular cars.
4. Compare two cities.
5. Compare your country to the United States.
6. Compare two popular teams.
7. Compare two airlines.
8. Compare two tv channels.
9. Compare two members of your family.

Grammar Focus

SHORT ANSWERS WITH INFINITIVES

We can use infinitives to give short answers.

Examples:
1. Why are you leaving?
   Because I want to.
2. Did you pay the phone bill?
   Oh, no! I forgot to.
3. Why does Michael work so many hours?
   Because he needs to.
4. Do you drink beer?
   I used to.
5. Have you called your mother?
   No, I haven't. But I'm going to.

Unit 6

Exercise 6.6

Answer the following questions. Use "Because I want to" or "Because I don't want to."

1. Why are you wearing that ugly jacket?
   _____.

2. Why aren't you going to cook?
   _____.

3. Why don't you go to school?
   _____.

4. Why are you going out with John?
   _____.

5. Why don't you have a baby?
   _____.

6. Why do you bother Kevin so much?
   _____.

7. Why aren't you in bed?
   _____.

8. Why do you work so much?
   _____.

9. Why don't you dye your hair?
   _____.

10. Why are you living with that silly man?
    _____.

Exercise 6.7

Answer the following questions. Use "I used to" or "I didn't use to."

1. You used to smoke when you were younger, right?
   No, _____.

2. Do you smoke?
   No, but _____.

3. Do you believe everything Angel says?
   Not anymore. But _____.

4. Didn't you use to work at Macy's?
   No, _____.

5. Are you married?
   No, I'm not. But _____.

Unit 6

Exercise 6.8

Answer the following questions. Choose an answer from the box.

I tried to	I want to	I have to
I'm trying to	I forgot to	I need to
I used to	I would love to	He didn't want to
I'm going to		

1. Did you turn off the lights?

    Oh, no! _____.

2. Did you do the homework?

    _____ but it was so difficult.

3. Why are you wearing those cheap pants?

    Because _____.

4. Why didn't Hector take his medicine?

    Because _____.

5. Why do you work at two jobs?

    Because _____.

6. Do you know how to play the guitar?

    No, but I _____.

7. Did you call your mother?

    Oh my God! _____, but I _____ right now.

Exercise 6.9

**Answer the following questions:
Use short answers with infinitives.**

1. Why don't you study more?

    Because I _____.

2. Are you going to the wedding?

    I _____ but I wasn't invited.

3. Did you do over the compositions?

   Oh, no! I _____ but I _____ right away.

4. Why are you wearing those ugly shoes?

   Because I _____.

5. Do you ever go dancing?

   Not anymore, but I _____.

6. Why didn't you make breakfast?

   Because I _____.

7. Did you stock the shelves?

   Oh, I didn't know I _____.

8. Did you pass the test?

   No, I didn't, but at least I _____.

Exercise 6.10

Answer the following questions:
Use short answers with Infinitives.

1. Do you play football?

   Not anymore, but I _____.

2. Do you call your family every day?

   Oh, I _____, but it's expensive.

3. Did you lock the door?

   Oh, I didn't know I _____.

4. Why is Rita moving out?

   Because she _____.

5. Why are Mr. and Mrs. White standing?

   I guess because they _____.

6. You sent the letter, right?

   Oh, no! I _____ but _____ right away.

7. Did you fix my car?

   No, we didn't. But we _____.

8. Would you like to go dancing tomorrow night?

   _____ but I can't.

Unit 6

9. Why aren't you going to clean the house today?

   Because _____.

10. Why is Sam getting married?

    Because he _____. His girlfriend is pregnant.

11. Are you going to the party?

    Well, I _____ if you invite me.

12. Are you going to study more?

    Of course I _____.

13. Why don't you pay attention?

    Because I _____.

14. Are you going to learn English perfectly?

    Well, _____.

15. Is Jim going back to work?

    _____ but the doctor told him not to.

Unit 6

Who's the best?

Reading

Ted Williams and John Miller have been friends most of their lives. They met back in 1985 when they were high school students and they've been good friends ever since.

When Ted got married, John was his best man at the wedding ceremony. Ted was also the best man on the day John finally decided to marry his high school sweetheart.

Even though Ted and John are good friends, they've always competed against each other. For instance, while in high school John used to get better grades than his friend Ted. Ted used to be more popular with girls.

When they graduated and started working they both got very good jobs. John was hired as an assistant manager at a large fast food restaurant chain and Ted began to work in the public relations department of a well-known company.

As you can see, both John and Ted are very successful people. Some of their friends and family tell them that competition among friends is not good, but they always reply with the same phrase: "We are not competing, we're just working our way up to the top together."

Comprehension Questions

1. What's this story about?
   Two friends.
   Competition.
   Successful people.
2. Do you have a friend like the one from the story?
3. What does "working one's way up to the top" mean?
4. Define the word success.

"Working ones way up to the top = Aiming for sucess

Unit 6

Grammar Focus

ADJECTIVES FOLLOWED BY INFINITIVES

(a) They were lucky to win the lottery.
(b) I was glad to see Mary at the party

Some adjectives can be immediately followed by Infinitives, as in (a) and (b). We use them to describe a person (or people), not things. Many of these adjectives describe a person's feelings or attitudes.

SOME COMMON ADJECTIVES FOLLOWED BY INFINITIVES

Afraid to	Delighted to	Likely to	Shocked to*
Amazed to*	Determined to	Lucky to	Sorry to*
Anxious to	Disappointed to*	Pleased to	Stunned to*
Ashamed to	Eager to	Prepared to	Surprised to*
Astonished to*	Fortunate to	Proud to	Upset to*
Careful to	Glad to	Ready to	Willing to
Certain to	Happy to	Relieved to	
Content to	Hesitant to	Sad to*	

*The expressions with asterisks are usually followed by infinitive phrases with verbs such as see, learn, discover, find out, hear.

Example: Rita was shocked to hear the news about her ex-boyfriend's death.

Unit 6

Exercise 6.11

Complete the sentences, using an expressions from Grammar Focus on page 108 and your own words. Give two possible responses.

Example:

Paul studies really hard.
<u>He's determined to be the best student in his class</u>.
<u>He's likely to get straight "A"'s on his finals</u>.

1. My friend just found out that his girlfriend is pregnant.

   He _____.

   He _____.

2. The crime rate in our city has increased enormously in the past 2 years.

   We _____.

   We _____.

3. I don't like my job.

   I'm _____.

   I'm _____.

4. I've worked a lot all day long.

   I think I'm _____.

   I think I'm _____.

5. I need a job desperately.

   I'm _____.

   I'm _____.

6. Claire's family is very loving and supportive.

   She's _____.

   She's _____.

7. My brother is always late for work.

   He's _____.

   He's _____.

8. You're having a test tomorrow. Are you prepared for it?

   Yes, I'm _____.

   Yes, I'm _____.

9. Sally told me what my girlfriend was up to while I was on vacation.

   I'm _____.

   I'm _____.

10. I managed to get tickets to the ballet. My friend Sara loves ballet.

    She's _____.

    She's _____.

Unit 6

Exercise 6.12 Pair Work

Speaker A: (your book is open). Ask questions.
Speaker B: (your book is closed).
Answer questions in complete sentences.

> **Example:**
>
> **Speaker A:**
> What are you careful to do before you leave your home?
>
> **Speaker B:**
> Before I leave my home I'm careful to.... **lock the doors.**
> .... **turn off the stove.** etc.

1. Sometimes when people don't speak English very well, what are they reluctant to do?

2. What are some things you would feel embarrassed to do?

3. If a friend has a big problem, what are you willing to do?

4. When you get a raise, what are you motivated to do?

5. Is there something you're eager to do today or tomorrow?

6. What are you sometimes afraid to do?

7. Do you remember something you were shocked to find out?

8. Do you remember something you were disappointed to discover?

9. Can you tell me something you were surprised to hear?

10. What are you determined to do before you are 65 years old?

Unit 6

Pronunciation Section

Grammar Discrimination

> "Can" is pronounced cən. The main verb is stressed.
>
> **She can sing well.**   **She cən síng well.**
>
> "Can't" is pronounced cǻnt. Usually we don't hear the **t**. Both "can't" and the main verb are stressed.
>
> **She can't sing well.**   **She cǻnt síng well.**

Exercise 6.13

A.   Practice the following words.

1. She can't close the door.
   cǻnt clóse

2. He can't type.
   cǻnt týpe

3. They can study and work.
   cən stúdy

4. Liz can drive fast.
   cən dríve

5. They can't pay their bills.
   cǻnt páy

B.   Write can or can't and the main verb that you hear.

1. They _____ _____ too well.

2. She _____ _____ Italian food.

3. They _____ _____ the apartment.

4. He _____ _____ the address.

5. She _____ _____ on vacation.

Unit 6

Big Cities vs. Small Towns

Reading

For reading and discussion.
Look at these two pictures.
Which place would you like to live in? Why?

Living in a big city

Some advantages of living in a big city are, with no doubt, more job opportunities, better services, good transportation, higher salaries, an outstanding nightlife and a better chance to enjoy art and leisure activities.

On the other hand issues such as high crime rate, pollution, and unsafe neighborhoods are to be taken into consideration before you decide to move to a place like this.

Living in a small town

Some advantages of living in a small town are, with no doubt, quieter and safer neighborhoods, friendlier people and less or no pollution.

However, issues such as fewer job opportunities, longer commuting time, reduced nightlife, infrequent transportation, and in many cases lower wages are to be taken into consideration before you decide to move to a place like this.

Comprehension Questions

1. Where would you rather live if:
    - you were married with children?
    - you were single?
    - you were a student?
    - you had just graduated from college?
2. What advantages and disadvantages does your city have? Explain.
3. Would you recommend somebody to come and live in this city?
4. If you had the power to change the quality of life in this city, what would you change? Explain.

UNIT 6 | 113

Unit 6

Writing

If possible, divide into groups of the same sex (women work with women and men work with men). In your group, make a list of the characteristics you think are most important in your ideal partner. What things do you need and what things do you want?

Compare lists. Do men and women want and need the same things? Why or why not?

What do men and women want?

UNIT 7

Content
- Gerunds
- Superlative Form of Adjectives and Adverbs

"I avoid *eating* at night"

01. COMMUNICATION **02. COMPREHENSION** **03. WRITING** **04. GRAMMAR**

Unit 7

I can't stand waiting for people.

Reading

Complete the paragraphs with these words:

resume	can't stand	deal with	kind of	proud of
qualities	positive	disappointed	solve	as good as

There are many good _____ about myself that I'm really _____. For instance, I love working hard, I like fixing things and I'm the _____ person who enjoys helping others with their problems.

People always come to me when they have a problem they can't _____. For example, just yesterday one of my best friends lost his job and he was very sad and _____. He said he would never be able to find another job _____ the one he had! It took me about thirty minutes to prepare his _____ and to make a few phone calls and before he knew it, he was working for one of the best computer companies in town.

There are many _____ qualities that I like about myself but there are also some things I just _____. For example, I don't like waiting in line at public service buildings, spending a lot of time by myself, people who talk too much or watching TV alone, but the one thing I just can't _____ _____ is waiting for people.

Comprehension Questions

Answer these questions in pairs or small groups. Explain your answers.

1. What are some of the positive qualities you have?
2. What are some of the negative ones?
3. Do you like helping people with their problems?
4. Who do you turn to when you have a problem?
5. Name three things you can't tolerate?

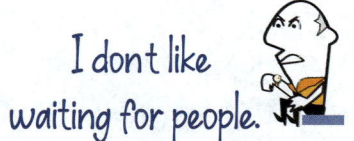

116 | INTERACTIONS

Unit 7

Grammar Focus

VERB + GERUND

Some verbs are followed by gerunds.

(a) I enjoy **talking** about politics. (b) My parents considered **moving** to California. (c) I avoid **eating** at night.	In (a), (b) and (c), gerunds are used as the object of the verbs "enjoy," "consider" and "avoid."

COMMON VERBS FOLLOWED BY GERUNDS:

Discuss	Finish	Consider
Quit	Stop	Enjoy
Mind	Avoid	Keep

For more verbs followed by a gerund, see Appendix 3

Exercise 7.1

Complete the sentences by using Gerunds. Add a preposition after the Gerund if necessary.

Example: When Peter finished <u>doing</u> his homework, he watched TV.

1. We discussed _____ Florida for our vacation.
2. I quit _____ two years ago.
3. Sometimes students put off _____ their homework.
4. I'm thinking about _____ my old car for a new.
5. Could you please stop _____ that? It's very annoying.
6. A: Are you listening to me?

   B: Yes, keep _____.
7. I'm considering _____ my class schedule.
8. I really enjoy _____ to the sound of rain on my window.
9. When you finish _____, could you come here and help me?
10. My mother discontinued _____ that face cream because it irritated her skin.

UNIT 7 | 117

Unit 7

Grammar Focus

VERB + INFINITIVE

Some verbs are followed by an infinitive:	
(a) My parents promised **to visit** me next year. (b) I want **to get** a new job.	**INFINITIVE** = to + simple form of a verb.
(c) My sister decided **not to study** medicine.	**Negative form:** not + infinitive.

COMMON VERBS FOLLOWED BY INFINITIVES:

Refuse	Appear	Hope	Plan
Want	Need	Promise	Learn (how)
Agree	Pretend	Mean	Offer

Exercise 7.2

Complete the sentences by using Infinitives from the box.

| to eat | to be | to see | to help | to buy | to talk |
| to fix | to go | to travel | to study | to go back | |

1. I can't afford _____ a new car this year.
2. My mother decided _____ to school and study English.
3. I can't wait _____ my friends at the party this Saturday.
4. John promised _____ more responsible in his job.
5. The baby refused _____ his food.
6. After I finish studying English I would like _____ German.
7. Mary wishes _____ to Florida on vacation this year.
8. I hope _____ you soon!
9. My friend Paul agreed _____ me with my homework.
10. The lawyer requested _____ to his client.
11. When I retire, I would like _____ around the world.
12. The man offered _____ my car for $200.

Unit 7

When the verb **to stop** has an infinitive after it, it means one thing, when it has a gerund after it, it means something else.

Example:

I stopped **to smoke**: I was driving my car and I stopped along the way to smoke a cigarrette.
I stopped **smoking**: After I spoke to the doctor about lung cancer, I stopped smoking.

Exercise 7.3

Underline the correct form of the verb as your teacher reads it to you.

1. She planned (to see, seeing) that TV program.
2. They're considering (to move, moving) to another town.
3. We finished (to work, working) at 5:00 p.m.
4. I can't help (to eat, eating) hamburgers and fries.
5. They prefer (to cook, cooking) their own meals.
6. Peter insists on (to go, going) by car.
7. They began (to study, studying) three hours ago.
8. Bob would like (to watch, watching) television, but he doesn't have time.
9. I enjoy (to eat, eating) spaghetti.
10. She kept on (thinking, to think) about the problem.

Exercise 7.4

Before you read.
-Do you like going on picnics?
-What do you do with your friends when you get together?
-What places do you enjoy visiting, eating at, etc?

How to prepare a picnic

When Ellen prepares for her annual picnic with her friends from work, she always writes a list of the things she will need or do.

This time they first thought about going to "Forrest Hill Park", but then they decided not to because they want to avoid driving that far especially on a Sunday morning when a lot of travelers are on the road. That's why this year Ellen and her friends talked about going to the Botanical Gardens located within the city limits.

She is also considering getting a new grill because the one she has is too old and rusty. They think about driving there instead of taking some other kind of public transportation because they want to enjoy being together without depending on bus schedules.

Ellen and her friends really enjoy planning their annual picnic on the same day and month every year and they never put it off unless it rains.

How to plan a party

Before you write
What would you take into consideration before planning a party?
How many people would you invite?
What kind of food would you suggest serving?
What kind of music would you enjoy listening to?

Unit 7

Guided Conversation

Read the model, and then answer the questions accordingly.

1. A: Where/go/next/weekend?
   B: Well, first I considered ....,
   but then I thought about...............
   finally, I decided to........................

What/do/next vacation?

A: What are you going to do on your next vacation?
B: Well, first I considered **going to Hawaii**, but then I thought about **visiting my uncle in Florida for a couple of days.** Finally, I decided to **stay home and rest.**

2. A: What/wear/for the party/tonight?
   B: red jacket/blue suit/brown shirt and khaki pants.

3. A: What/buy/your mother/her birthday?
   B: pearl necklace/gold ring/new dress.

4. A: Where/take/wife/anniversary?
   B:..

5. A: What/movie/watch/tomorrow night?
   B:..

6. A: What/cook/dinner/tonight?
   B:..

7. A: What/book/read/this week?
   B:..

8. A: What/job/get/this summer?
   B:..

9. A: What/do/next/day off?
   B:..

10. On your own

Unit 7

My Weakest Subject of Them All

Two friends are talking about school subjects and preferences.

Steve: I can hardly wait for school to finish!

Mike: Yeah, me too! These finals are driving me crazy, especially mathematics and geography.

Steve: Tell me about it. I think mathematics is the most difficult subject.

Mike: No doubt about it. Which is your easiest subject? Mine is geography.

Steve: Mine is definitely English. My teacher always tells me that I'm the best student she has.

Mike: You're lucky. English is my weakest subject of them all.

Steve: Let's make a deal. I'll help you study so you can get a high score on your English test if you promise to help me with geography.

Mike: You've got yourself a deal!!

Unit 7

Grammar Focus

SUPERLATIVE FORM OF ADJECTIVES: Using –est and most.

(a) My brother is **the tallest** of my family.
(b) Eric is **the most intelligent** student in my class.
(c) Kate is **the most beautiful** girl in my neighborhood.

The superlative form of adjectives compare more than two people, places or things.

	ADJECTIVE	COMPARATIVE	SUPERLATIVE
One syllable adjectives	Old	Older	The oldest
	Short	Shorter	The shortest
	High	Higher	The highest
	Hard	Harder	The hardest
One syllable adjectives ending in vowel and consonant	Big	Bigger	The biggest
	Hot	Hotter	The hottest
	Fat	Fatter	The fattest
	Thin	Thinnest	The thinnest
Two syllables adjectives that end in -Y	Pretty	Prettier	The prettiest
	Easy	Easier	The easiest
	Heavy	Heavier	The heaviest
Adjectives with two or more syllables	Interesting	More interesting	The most interesting
	Important	More important	The most important
	Beautiful	More beautiful	The most beautiful
	Difficult	More difficult	The most difficult
Irregular forms	Good	Better	The best
	Bad	Worse	The worst
	Far	Farther/further	The farthest/furthest

Note: - Use comparatives to compare two people, places, or things.
- Use superlatives to compare more than two people, places, or things.

Remember:
The superlative form of all adjectives and adverbs is preceded by: <u>the</u>

The North Pole is the coldest place in the world.

Unit 7

Exercise 7.5

Supply the superlative form of the Adjective or Adverb in parenthesis. Be sure to use the Article the.

1. What's _____ (good) savings bank in the city?
2. She's _____ (intelligent) person I know.
3. I don't like to drive on this road. It's _____ (dangerous) road in the state.
4. December is _____ (nice) month of the year.
5. The Roma is _____ (good) restaurant in town.
6. These exercises are_____(difficult) in the book.
7. Which is _____(good) route from New York to Miami?
8. The New York Times is _____(important) newspaper in town.
9. Peter is _____(bad) student in the class.
10. My father is _____(intelligent) person I know.
11. History is_____(easy) subject at school.
12. New York is _____(cosmopolitan) city in the world.

Exercise 7.6

A.- Personalization. What's your opinion? Fill out the survey about your city or town.

The best restaurant	
The best bank	
The cheapest supermarket	
The nicest hotel	
The most expensive clothing store	

B.- Discussion. Compare opinions with your classmates. Follow the model.

A: Which is *the best restaurant* in town?
B: In my opinion _____ is the best restaurant in town.
A: Why do you think so?
B: Because _____.

Unit 7

Exercise 7.7

The Best And The Worst About My Country.

1. Class Survey:

    A- Roam around the class and ask three people about their country of origin.

    B- Ask questions such as:

        1.   Where do you come from?

        2.   How long did you live there?

        3.   What's the best point about living in your country?

        4.   What's the worst point about it?

2. Complete the following chart:

NAME	COUNTRY	BEST	WORST

    C- Report back to the class.
    D- Follow the model.

Victor is from *Mexico*.

He lived there until he was 20 years old.

He says the best point about living in his country is that *"Education is free and mandatory for everybody."*

He also said that the worst point was *that some cities were very dirty and polluted*.

Exercise 7.8

Put a check mark in the parenthesis (√) by the correct Superlative Form of the Adjective.

Example:
( ) Carefulest   (√) The most beautiful   ( ) The happier

1. ( ) bigger
2. ( ) the most important
3. ( ) the nicest
4. ( ) the better
5. ( ) more far

6. ( ) the baddest
7. ( ) necesarier
8. ( ) the most intelligent
9. ( ) the most busy
10. ( ) the most rapidly

11. ( ) the saddest
12. ( ) the most
13. ( ) the quickest
14. ( ) the goodest
15. ( ) the most elegant

Exercise 7.9

A. The box below has Adjectives and Adverbs. Choose 15 and place them in the chart writing the Comparative and Superlative Forms under each word.
Follow the example in number 1.

ADJECTIVES AND ADVERBS

Modern	Expensive	Comfortable	Dull
Smooth	Heavy	Deep	Bad
Intelligent	Late	High	Good
Cheap	Quiet	Strong	Fast
Warm	Dangerous	Old	Nice
Young	Quick	Difficult	Cold
Noisy	Friendly	Salty	Slowly

1. cheap / cheaper / the cheapest	2.	3.	4.	5.
6.	7.	8.	9.	10.
11.	12.	13.	14.	15.

B. Work with a partner. Say your number two. Your partner should say the Comparative and Superlative Forms without looking at the book. If his or her answer is correct, say, "that's right." If it's not correct, say, "No, try again."

Unit 7

Exercise 7.10

Read each sentence carefully.
If the underlined part is correct, circle the word CORRECT.
If it's not, circle the word WRONG.

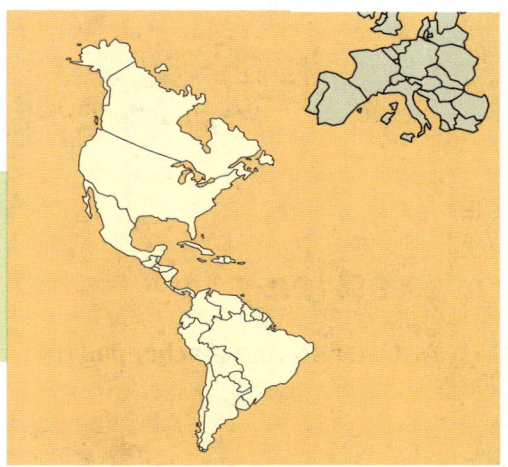

Example:
1. correct ~~wrong~~   America is <u>the smallest than</u> Europe.

2. correct   wrong   Which car is <u>the most expensiver</u>?

3. correct   wrong   Do you know the name of <u>the most famous</u> movie star alive?

4. correct   wrong   The smell of garlic is <u>more stronger than</u> the smell of onions.

5. correct   wrong   English <u>is the easier</u> language to learn.

6. correct   wrong   Today will be <u>the coldest</u> day of the year.

7. correct   wrong   The statue of Liberty is <u>the most famous than</u> the Eiffel Tower.

8. correct   wrong   "Let's buy this cake." It looks <u>the most delicious than</u> the other one.

9. correct   wrong   She is <u>more gooder than</u> her sister.

10. correct   wrong   Liz didn't eat breakfast today, so of course she's <u>hungrier than</u> I am.

11. correct   wrong   Paul is <u>the smartest</u> student in his class.

12. correct   wrong   Peter is <u>lazier than</u> Mark.

13. correct   wrong   Reading a magazine is <u>more interesting than</u> reading a history book.

14. correct   wrong   I am not <u>the tallest</u> in my family. My brother is.

15. correct   wrong   Paying for things by check is <u>the most covenient than</u> paying in cash.

Unit 7

Pronunciation Section

Emphatic Stress

> We put a higher pitch and additional stress on words that we want to emphasize.

Exercise 7.11

A. Listen to your teacher and then practice the following sentences.

I think it's **boring** to watch a movie by yourself.

I **hate** it when people lie to me.
I **love** to go shopping with my best friend.
I can't **stand** waiting in line at the bank.

B. Mark the emphatic stress in these sentences. Compare your sentences with a partner.

1. It bothers me when somebody knocks on my door at 2:00 a.m.
2. I think it's disgusting when people spit on the floor.
3. I think it's wonderful to hear from an old friend.
4. It really upsets me when my girlfriend is late.
5. It embarrasses me when my boss corrects me in front of others.

Unit 7

A Family Tradition

Lake Tahoe

Reading

WARM-UP QUESTIONS

1. What's a family tradition?
2. Does your family have a tradition?
3. Do you like camping?
4. What's your favorite camping spot?

Mike and Fred are planning a camping trip to Lake Tahoe this weekend. They've gone camping there every year for the past six years since they graduated from high school.

This year their friends Ann Barclay and Linda Jensen as well as Fred's youngest brother, Little Joe, are going along with them.

They say it is always nice to get out of the city at least for a couple of days, especially during the holidays.

Although it is a long ride, they love going to Tahoe and they usually stop a few times to look at the breathtaking scenery and eat at some of the nice outdoor restaurants they find along the way.

"Some day," Fred says," when we get married and have our own children we will also take them camping to Lake Tahoe. It'll become a family tradition to see the beautiful sunrise and to roast marshmallows on an open fire."

Comprehension Questions

1. Summarize the story.
2. Mike and Fred are:
   a. good friends.   b. brothers.   c. high school students.
3. Where are they planning a camping trip to?
4. How long ago did they graduate from high school?
5. Who are they taking with them this time?

Unit 7

Writing

Write a short story about a tradition in your own family.

UNIT 8

Content
- Tag Questions
- Causative Verbs
- Verbs of Perception

"Joe can speak English, can't he?"

01. COMMUNICATION   **02. COMPREHENSION**   **03. WRITING**   **04. GRAMMAR**

Unit 8

It's a beautiful day, isn't it?

Reading

Agnes: It's a beautiful day, isn't it?

Sophia: Yes, it is. I really enjoy walking in the park on such lovely days.

Agnes: Why don't we stop for a cup of coffee on our way back home? There's a small cafeteria next to the subway station. You still drink coffee, don't you?

Sophia: No, I don't. I stopped drinking coffee since my doctor told me to do so two months ago.

Agnes: Then we'll both have a cup of tea and a thick slice of their famous chocolate cake.

Sophia: You were on diet before, weren't you?

Agnes: I was, but not anymore. Let's go to the cafeteria. Tomorrow will be a beautiful day to walk in the park, too, won't it?

Sophia: Of course it will!!

Comprehension Questions

Answer and discuss these questions.

1. How old do you think Agnes and Sophia are?
2. Why do they walk in the park?
3. Is walking a good exercise?
4. How often do you walk as an exercise?
5. What's another way to keep yourself in shape?
6. Why do you think Agnes and Sophia are coming back to the park tomorrow?

Unit 8

Grammar Focus

TAG QUESTIONS

A Tag Question is a question added at the end of a sentence. We use tag questions to make sure our information is correct, to seek agreement or invite confirmation of some fact we already know.

Example:
(a) Joe can speak English, **can't he?**
(b) Fred can't drive, **can he?**
(c) You like tea, **don't you?**

* tag endings contain a pronoun and an auxiliary verb, but not a main verb.

A positive sentence	a negative tag question
Lisa is happy,	isn't she?
You like coffee,	don't you?
They will come,	won't they?

A negative sentence	a positive tag question
Lisa isn't happy,	is she?
You don't like coffee,	do you?
They won't come,	will they?

(a) **This/that** is your car, isn't **it**? (b) **These/those** are your books, aren't **they**?	The tag pronoun for **this/that = it** The tag pronoun for **these/those = they**
(c) **There** is a party tonight, isn't **there**? (d) **Everything** is O.K, **isn't it**? (e) **Everyone** took the test, **didn't they**?	In the sentence there + be; there is used in the tag. Personal pronouns are used to refer to indefinite pronouns. **They** is usually used in a tag to refer to **everyone, everybody, someone, somebody, no one, nobody.**
(f) **Nothing** is wrong, **is it**? (g) **Nobody** came, **did they**? (h) **You've never** gone there, **have you**?	Sentences with negative words take affirmative tags.
(i) **I am** supposed to be here, **am I not**? (j) **I am** supposed to be here, **aren't I**?	In (i): **am I not?** is formal English In (j): **aren't I?** Is common in spoken English.

* **Am I not?** is most likely to be used in England rather than in America, as well as in more formal situations of speech.

Unit 8

Exercise 8.1

Add the appropriate Tag Questions to the following.

1. They don't want to come, _____?
2. George is a doctor, _____?
3. They won't arrive on time, _____?
4. There aren't any problems, _____?
5. That is your pencil, _____?
6. She has worked a lot in the last couple of days, _____?
7. Everyone can learn how to speak English, _____?
8. Nobody cheated on the exam, _____?
9. She has a new bike, _____?
10. You've never been to London, _____?
11. He'll help you later, _____?
12. I am not invited, _____?

Exercise 8.2 Oral (Books Closed)

Add Tag Questions.

> A: (Peter) is a mechanic ....
>
> B: Response: ....isn't he?

1. You didn't forget your books.......
2. There isn't a test tomorrow ....
3. (.....) is going to come to class tomorrow ....
4. (.....) lives on (Main street) ....
5. (.....) can't speak (Spanish) ....
6. (.....) doesn't have a car ....

Unit 8

7. I am right ....

8. (.....) is never late to class ....

9. (.....) sat next to (.....) yesterday ....

10. You used to live in New York ....

11. We have class tomorrow ....

12. You haven't done your laundry this week.......

Exercise 8.3

Complete the sentences with a negative or positive Tag Question.

You don't have a car, _____?   No, I can't drive.

The movie wasn't good, _____?   No, It was boring.

You will help me, _____?   Yes, of course I will.

You play soccer, _____?   Yes, but not often.

You can swim, _____?   Yes, but not very well.

He looks very tired, _____?   Yes, he works very hard.

Unit 8

Pronunciation Section

Emphatic Stress

> Intonation in Tag Questions
>
> - **A tag question may be spoken:**
>
> - With a rising intonation if the speaker is truly seeking to ascertain that his/her information, idea or belief is correct.
>   Example: Lisa lives in Paterson, doesn't she?
>
> - With a falling intonation if the speaker is expressing an idea with which s/he is almost sure the listener will agree.
>   Example: It's a nice day today, isn't it?

Exercise 8.4

A. Practice Intonation in Tag Questions.

Use rising or falling intonation. (Draw the appropriate arrow) ↘ or ↗.

1. Life is difficult in the United States, **isn't it?**
2. There isn't enough gun control in this city, _____?
3. AIDS is a global crisis, _____?
4. Unemployment is not a major problem in this country, _____?
5. Illiteracy is the name of a book, _____?
6. Health insurance is very cheap, _____?
7. Scientists shouldn't use animals for research, _____?
8. There aren't enough days in the week, _____?

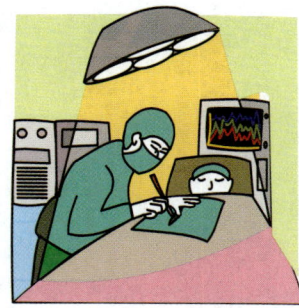

B. **Pair Work**

Take turns reading the statements with Tag Questions from the exercise above.

Give your own opinion when responding.

Unit 8

A Bad Hair Day

Reading

Sarah: Hello! Is that you, Helen?
Helen: Yes, Sarah, I'm so glad you called me. Tonight's the big party and my hair is a mess. Do you know where I can get it done on such short notice?
Sarah: Let me think... I know a woman who works at a good hair salon, but you'd need to make an appointment at least two days in advance.
Helen: What if you call her up, and get her to do my hair this afternoon? Would you do that for me, pleeease!

Exercise 8.5

What happened afterwards?

Work in pairs and think of a possible ending for the conversation.

_____
_____
_____
_____
_____
_____
_____
_____
_____

Grammar Focus

USING CAUSATIVE VERBS: MAKE, HAVE and GET.

We use causative verbs to express the idea that the subject "X" causes someone else "Y", to perform an action, or do something.

(a) I **made** my brother **do** my laundry. X makes Y do something. (simple form)
(b) I **had** my brother **do** my laundry. X has Y do something. (simple form)
(c) I **got** my brother **to do** my laundry. X gets Y to do something. (infinitive)

When: **make, have** and **get**, are used as causative verbs, their meanings are similar but not identical. In **(a)**: My brother had no choice. I insisted that he do my laundry. In **(b)** My brother did my laundry simply because I asked him to. In **(c)**: I managed to persuade my brother to do my laundry.

(d) My boss **made** me work overtime.

The simple form of a verb follows causative make. Make gives the idea that "X" forces "Y" to do something. In **(d)** I had no choice.

(e) I **had** the mechanic **fix** my car.
(f) Joan **had** the teacher **correct** her homework.

Causative have is followed by the simple form of a verb. **Have** gives the idea that "X" requests "Y" to do something. In **(e)**: The teacher corrected my homework because Joan asked her to.

(g) Joe **got** his father **to lend** him the car.
(h) I **got** my sister **to clean** my room.

Causative get is followed by an infinitive. **Get** gives the idea that "X" persuades "Y" to do something. In **(g)**: Joe managed to persuade his father to lend him his car.

Unit 8

Exercise 8.6

Finish the sentence.

Example:
Sometimes I get my friend Jack.......to do my homework.

1. Sometimes parents make their children ....
2. Teachers often have their students ....
3. We had a professional photographer ....
4. Alice had her sister ....
5. When I'm at a restaurant, I sometimes have the waiter ....
6. Peeling onions always makes me ....
7. The dentist made the patient ....
8. I made my little brother ....
9. My boss made me ....
10. I finally got my landlord ....

Exercise 8.7

Complete the sentences with the word in parenthesis.

Example: I had a bad headache yesterday, so I got my mother to call my boss and explain to him my absence.

1. The dentist made the patient (open) _____ her mouth.
2. The teacher had the class (repeat) _____ the word ten times.
3. I got my brother (lend) _____ me his portable C.D player.
4. Waiting for people always makes me (angry) _____.
5. We had a professional photographer (take) _____ pictures at the baby's birthday party.
6. I went to the bank to have a check (cash) _____.
7. My boss made me (call) _____ the client three times.
8. I made my son (clean) _____ his room, before he could go outside and play.
9. I need to get my suit (clean) _____ before the job interview.
10. Mike took his car to the repair shop to have it (fix) _____.

Unit 8

Pronunciation Section

Sentence Stress

Notice the sentence stress in these active and passive sentences:

Active
A: Where can I have someone fix my **car**?
B: You can have someone **fix** it at **Joe's** Auto Repair Shop.
Passive
A: Where can I have my **car** fixed?
B: You can have it **fixed** at **Joe's** Auto Repair Shop.

Exercise 8.8 Group Work

Ask questions about things you want to have done.
Remember the sentence stress. Other students give answers.

Example:
A: Where can I have a jacket **altered**?
B: You can have it **altered** at Jimmy's tailoring shop.

Grammar Focus

CAUSATIVE VERBS   Passive Voice

(a) I **had** my hair **cut** (by someone). (b) I **got** my hair **cut** (by someone).	The past participle is used after **have** and **get** to give a passive meaning and to say that we have arranged for someone else to do something for us. In this case there is little difference between both verbs. In **(a)** and **(b)**: I caused my hair to be cut by someone.

* **The word order is important:** Notice that the past participle (painted, fixed, taken, etc.) comes after the object (his house, your car, etc.)

Unit 8

	have/get +	object +	past participle	
Bill	had	his house	painted	yesterday.
Where did you	get	your car	fixed?	
We are	having	our picture	taken	right now.
Sally has just	had	her hair	cut	by her friend.
How often do you	get	your lawn	mow?	
Why don't you	have	your suit	dry cleaned?	
She wants to	have	her nails	done.	

Get something done by someone is possible instead of have something done by someone (mainly in informal spoken English).

* I think you should get your hair cut (by someone).
* I think you should have your hair cut (by someone).

Exercise 8.9

Answer the questions as in the example.

Example:
"Did you paint your house yourself?" "No, <u>I had it painted.</u>

1. "Did James mow the lawn himself?"   "No, he _____."

2. "Did Susan make the cake herself?"   "No, she _____."

3. "Did they paint the house themselves?"   "No, they _____."

4. "Did Frank cut his hair himself?"   "No, he _____."

5. "Did Martha wash the car herself?"   "No, she _____."

Unit 8

Exercise 8.10

Finish the sentences. Use the words in parenthesis.

1. Your lawn is too high. I think you should _____(it/mow).
2. The car has a strange noise. You should _____(it/repair).
3. A. What is that man doing on your roof?

   B. Oh, I _____(it/fix).
4. How often _____(your house/paint).
5. _____(your groceries/deliver) or do you buy them yourself at the store?
6. How_____(your hair/ do)?
7. My nails look horrible! I need to_____

   as soon as possible. (them/ polish).
8. How often _____(the carpet, clean)?
9. How often_____(your basement, clean)?
10. A: What are those men doing in your yard?

    B: Oh, I_____. (a swimming pool , build).

Unit 8

Guided Conversation

A. PAIR WORK

You want to have these things done. Write questions using the passive with get or have. Then write possible answers.

Example:
have someone wash my car.

A: **Where** can I **have my car washed?**
B: You could **have it washed at Mike's car wash.**

1. have someone read my fortune.

2. get a professional to teach me about computers.

3. have someone walk my dog.

4. get my roommate to do my laundry.

5. have someone wash my car.

6. have someone check my heart.

7. have someone fix my tv set.

8. get my father to lend me his car.

9. On your own.

B. **PAIR WORK**
   Take turns asking and answering the questions. Start your conversation like this:
   Do you know where I can.................?
   Do you know how I can ....?

Do you know where I can have my dog groomed?

You could have it groomed by my cousin. She's a pet's groomer!

Grammar Focus

Using And Understanding VERBS OF PERCEPTION		
Verbs of perception are verbs we use to perceive things through our senses: touch, sight, smell and ear.		
Some verbs of perception are followed by either **the simple form** or **the -ing form** of a verb. There is **no difference** between the two forms except that the **–ing** form gives the idea of **"while"**.		
(a) I **saw** my teacher **walk** down the street. **(b)** I **saw** my teacher **walking** down the street. **(c)** I **heard** the bird **sing** in the tree. **(d)** I **heard** the bird **singing** in the tree.		In **(b)** I saw my teacher **while** he was walking down the street In **(d)** I heard the bird **while** it was singing in the tree.
Sometimes there is a **clear difference** between the simple form and the –ing form.		
(e) I **heard** Mozart's Ninth Symphony last night.		In **(e)** I heard the symphony **from beginning to end**.
(f) When I walked into the class today, I **heard** a student **talking** about the weather.		In **(f)** the speech **was in progress** when I heard it.
*The simple form of a verb = The infinitive form without "to".		

Unit 8

Incorrect:
I saw my teacher **to walk** down the street.

Correct:
I saw my teacher **walk** down the street.

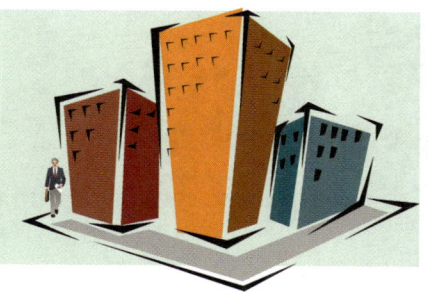

VERBS OF PERCEPTION FOLLOWED BY THE SIMPLE FORM OR THE ING FORM				
See	Hear	Feel	Smell	Observe
Notice	Listen to	Watch	Look at	

Exercise 8.11

In the following practice, choose the most appropriate form of the verbs in parenthesis. (either simple or -ing).

1. Last night I went to a jazz concert at the National Auditorium. I really enjoyed watching the musicians _____ their instruments. (play)

2. Do you see Tom _____ up that hill? Isn't that him, the tall man in the blue jacket. (run)

3. When I woke up this morning, I saw some birds _____ on my window sill. (stand)

4. Do you hear someone _____ in the next room? Yes, I do. (sing)

5. When I looked out the window, I saw the thief _____ to jump over the fence. (try)

6. When Joe heard the teacher _____ his name. He walked towards the board. (call)

7. As soon as we walked into the house, we smelled something _____. (burn)

8. Last night when Jack was watching television, he heard his neighbors _____. (argue)

9. While I was waiting for my pizza, I watched other people _____ theirs. (eat)

10. Timmy was working in the garage, so he didn't hear his mother _____ for lunch. (call)

11. When I was at the Bank yesterday, I saw the police _____ a suspicious man. (arrest)

12. As soon as Mary saw her father _____ of the car, she gave him a big hug and a kiss. (step out)

UNIT 8 | 145

Unit 8

Exercise 8.12

Verbs of Perception.

Finish these sentences with an appropriate form (either simple or -ing) of a verb.

Example:

While I was on vacation in the countryside,
I loved to hear the birds **singing** every morning.

1. I was almost asleep last night when I suddenly heard something _____ from one of the cabinets in the kitchen.

2. I was watching TV, so I didn't feel you _____. You scared me!

3. On my way to work, I always observe an old woman _____ the birds with breadcrumbs.

4. I like to listen to my father _____ his guitar. He's such a good guitarist.

5. We like to watch the chef _____ the bread.

Unit 8

Reading

1. Have you ever been mugged?
2. If so, What happened?
3. Did you call the police?
4. What did you tell them?

Statistics say that the average person will be robbed or mugged at least twice in his or her lifetime.

Is your city a safe place to live?
Are your children safe at school?
Is there anything you as a citizen can do to prevent crime?

These and more are questions you have probably asked yourself and your friends. Our cities are growing so fast that it is very difficult for us not to be victims of crime or robbery at least once in our lives.

If you or somebody you know has been a victim of a crime or has witnessed a crime there are some important steps you have to follow in order to help the police find and charge the muggers.

Report the crime immediately.
Call the police in the town in which the crime occurred, not the town you live in.
Try to remember as many details as you can.
If there is a car involved try to get the license plate number.
Write down as many details as possible.

Serious crime will continue to happen in our cities, but taking some precautions and being alert are two very good ways to fight against it. BE SAFE!

Writing

A friend of yours is planning to move into town with his family.

Since they've always lived in a rural area they are not very familiar with life in a big city. Write him a letter about some precautions he and his family should take into consideration before coming here. (Use the space provided.)

UNIT 9

Content
- Adjectives Ending in ED & ING
- Synonyms
- Antonyms

"The news was shocking"

01. COMMUNICATION **02. COMPREHENSION** **03. WRITING** **04. GRAMMAR**

Unit 9

Grandpa Joe the "Storyteller"

Reading

His real name is Joseph, but everybody has always called him "Joe" since he was young. He is my father's father, and he is an *interesting* man. His life has been very *exciting*. When he was twenty-one years old, he convinced his mother, Dorothy, to let him get a job as a crew member on a merchant ship and sail around the world.

To his mother, the idea seemed *terrifying*, but since she was an *understanding* mother and Joe was such a good son, she had no choice but to let him do his will.

My grandfather sailed the seven seas for over twenty years and the stories he tells are *fascinating* as well as *exciting*.

"Once," he said, "A giant whale hit our ship, and we were about to sink in the north Atlantic. Another time, we were shocked to learn that we had run out of fuel 250 nautical miles from the coast of Africa." His stories can be a little confusing sometimes. I even think that some of them might not be true, but they are so interesting, convincing and amazing that I feel very fortunate to have a grandfather such as Joe "the storyteller."

Comprehension Sentences

Match the adjectives in column A with the nouns in column B to form collocations.
Example: "*convincing* idea"

A	B
a. convincing	1. story
b. shocked	2. news
c. terrifying	3. mother
d. pleasing	4. idea
e. confusing	5. to learn
f. excited	6. to go

Unit 9

Grammar Focus

ADJECTIVES ENDING IN -ED AND -ING

(a) Gina thinks that her *life* is bor**ing**.
 (b) *The movie* was interest**ing**.
 (c) *I* was worri**ed** about the test.
 (d) *Gina* is bor**ed** with her life.
	In English we can use **-ing** and **-ed** endings to form adjectives.
	 Example: - excit**ing** /excit**ed**
	               - bor**ing** / bor**ed**
	               - interest**ing** / interest**ed**... etc

(e) *The new professor* is bor**ing**. (f) *The book* is very bor**ing**.	▸ Adjectives ending in "**- ing**" can describe a person or thing. As in **(e)** and **(f)**.
(g) *I* am bor**ed** today. (h) *My aunt* was very confus**ed** yesterday.	▸ Adjectives ending in "**-ed**" describe a feeling. As in **(g)** and **(h)**.

Study these examples:

1. I was **shocked** at the news. The news was **shocking**.
2. A: Are you **interested** in astrology?
 B: No, I am not. I think astrology is **boring**.
3. Even though I enjoy my job, it is kind of **tiring**.
4. Do you get **embarrassed** easily?
5. Mark works fifty to sixty hours a week. By the end of the week he's **exhausted**.
6. The book was **boring**. It made me feel **bored**.

Someone is <u>**bored**</u> because something (or someone) is <u>**boring.**</u>

Exercise 9.1

Choose the correct form of the Adjective.

1. We were (**excited** / **exciting**) about the party.
2. The baseball game was very (**excited** / **exciting**).
3. The directions to the party were very (**confused, confusing**).
4. I was very (**confused, confusing**) with the directions.
5. Astronomy is an (**interested** / **interesting**) subject to teach.
6. I am (**interested** / **interesting**) in learning about computers.
7. I enjoy talking to Franco. He is very (**interested** / **interesting**).
8. The story was (**fascinated, fascinating**).
9. Larry thinks Art is (**bored** / **boring**).
10. My little sister is (**terrified** / **terrifying**) when she watches horror movies.
11. Learning to speak a second language is a (**satisfied** / **satisfying**) experience.
12. This room is (**disgusted** / **disgusting**), please clean it up.

Unit 9

Exercise 9.2

Choose the correct statement that best <u>describes</u> the underlined word(s).

1. I love to listen to <u>romantic songs</u>.
   a. They are **fascinated**.
   b. They are **fascinating**.
2. We have always planned special events on <u>my father</u>'s birthday.
   a. He is always **surprised**.
   b. He is always **surprising**.
3. <u>Linda</u> doesn't like to see her son skateboard on the street.
   a. She is **worried** about him.
   b. She is **worrying** about him.
4. Despite not saving any money, the <u>Richards</u> have bought a new h
   a. They were **amazed** to do that.
   b. They were **amazing** to do that.

5. All the students in <u>Professor Kane</u>'s history class failed their mid-term exams.
   a. She was **disappointed**.
   b. She was **disappointing**.
6. Keith enjoys <u>mountain biking</u> in the summer.
   a. It is an **amused** activity.
   b. It is an **amusing** activity.
7. Larry heard about the <u>train disaster</u> yesterday.
   a. It was **horrified** news.
   b. It was **horrifying** news.
8. Paul and Frank don't like to eat <u>spicy food</u>.
   a. For them it's **disgusted**.
   b. For them it's **disgusting**.
9. My stepmother enjoyed the <u>Broadway show</u> very much.
   a. It was **excited**.
   b. It was **exciting**.

10. Pluto is so mysterious and wondrous for <u>me</u>.
    a. I am **fascinated** with it.
    b. I am **fascinating** with it.
11. <u>Carl</u> never studied for his exams, but he passed all of them.
    a. He was **surprised**.
    b. He was **surprising**.
12. <u>That film</u> was extremely sad.
    a. It was really **depressed**.
    b. It was really **depressing**.

Unit 9

Exercise 9.3

Error Analysis. Adjectives with ed & -ing
Some sentences have mistakes and some don't. Correct the mistakes.

1. Angel and Patrick are dedicating workers.
   _____.

2. I enjoyed the science fiction movie because it was excited.
   _____.

3. We were horrified to hear the news about the hurricane in Puerto Rico.
   _____.

4. The singer has a fascinated voice.
   _____.

5. I can't stand watching soap operas because they're depressing.
   _____.

6. My father was disappointing with our performance in the game.
   _____.

7. Her hypocrisy is shocked to me because there is always a double standard when it comes to the rules at work.
   _____.

8. It's sometimes embarrassed to see them fall on the ice.
   _____.

9. She's worrying about the exam, because she isn't prepared.
   _____.

10. I am seldom amazing with the news.
    _____.

11. Paul ordered that astonishing new workout equipment.
    _____.

12. This exercise is exhausted.
    _____.

13. Billy and Marlene tried to save the frightening kittens.
    _____.

14. It was surprised that she won the beauty pageant.
    _____.

Unit 9

I'm bored with my boring job!

Reading

Doris has been a librarian most of her life. Since she became a librarian, she has done the same things every day and she's tired of it. Every day she has to file books and reference material, teach people how to use the Internet services her library offers, fill out library cards and call people at their homes when they forget to take books back to the library.

After sixteen years as a librarian, Doris is exhausted and ready to move on to a different job that is more challenging and rewarding.

Marcus has been a bus driver most of his life. Since he became a bus driver, he has done the same things every day and he's tired of it. Every day he has to greet his passengers, hand in bus tickets, announce bus stops through the passenger address system and drive his bus back to the garage in the evening.

After sixteen years as a bus driver, Marcus is exhausted and ready to move on to a different job that is more challenging and rewarding.

Comprehension Sentences

1. Find and circle the adjectives ending in **-ed** or **-ing**.
2. What is Doris tired of?
3. What is Marcus tired of?

"Help! I need a new job"

Unit 9

Guided Conversation

Follow the model.

A: Do you like _____?
(Definitely / Not Really). I think (it's/they're) ____.
A: How long have you felt that way?
B: I have been _____ by _____ for a long while.

Modern art (Fascinate)

A: *Do you like* <u>modern art</u>?
B: Definitely. I think it's really <u>fascinating</u>.
A: *How long have you felt that way?*
B: I have been <u>fascinated</u> by modern art for a long while.

1. Rock Music.
(Annoy)

2. Camping.
(Please)

3. History.
(Interest)

4. Mike's new dog.
(Frighten)

5. The company annual picnic.
(Excite)

6. Your baby pictures.
(Embarrass)

7. Mathematics
(Confuse)

8. Horror Movies.
(Terrify)

9. Driving a truck.
(Bore)

10. On your own.

Unit 9

Grammar Focus

SYNONYMS AND ANTONYMS

(a)	The driver **sped up** the car. The driver **accelerated** the car.	**Synonyms** are words that have the same or similar meaning even though they are written differently. Look at the following sets of words, they are synonyms.
(b)	She's a **careful** driver. She's a **cautious** driver.	
(c)	My teacher is very **slim**. My teacher is very **thin**.	(a) sped up - accelerated (b) careful - cautious (c) slim - thin
(d)	My friend Mike is very **smart**. On the other hand, my friend Ted is very **dumb**.	**Antonyms** are words that mean the opposite. Look at the following sets of words, they are antonyms.
(e)	Tina's skin is very **smooth**. On the other hand, Linda's skin is very **rough**.	
(f)	A: I really **enjoy** watching scary movies. B: My brother **dislikes** seeing scary movies.	(d) smart - dumb (e) smooth - rough (f) enjoy - dislike

SYNONYMS
1. Continue - Keep on
2. Smart   - Intelligent
3. Smooth   - Soft
4. Brave   - Courageous
5. Sick   - ill

ANTONYMS
1. Thin   - Obese
2. Careful - Careless
3. Arrive   - Depart
4. Give   - Receive
5. Love   - Hate

Exercise 9.1

Do you know the synonyms of these words?

1. Big _____
2. Great _____
3. Difficult _____
4. Boring _____
5. Distant _____

6. Errors _____
7. Tired _____
8. Worried _____
9. Begin _____
10. Scream _____

Unit 9

Exercise 9.5

Choose the Synonym of each underlined word(s) in the sentences.

1. The mailman **sobbed** when he heard the terrible news.
    a. cried
    b. lied

2. I couldn't listen to the cassette because it was **missing**.
    a. found
    b. lost

3. We have been learning the **sounds** for each verb.
    a. speech pattern
    b. music

4. William and Marlene **rushed** to work because they were late.
    a. hurried
    b. worried

5. I told Lynda that she had made an **error** with the score of the game.
    a. correction
    b. mistake

6. We are very **concerned** about our nephew Willie.
    a. proud
    b. worried

7. We must be **quiet** in the library because there are people reading there.
    a. noisy
    b. silent

8. David and Irma always watched Wrestling on TV because it was **amusing**.
    a. funny
    b. boring

9. My teacher would always get upset when I was **tardy** to class.
   a. on time
   b. late

10. Your sister-in-law has a **buddy** in San Diego.
    a. friend
    b. cousin

11. The classes exchanged **gifts** for Christmas.
    a. things
    b. presents

12. He always keeps his apartment **tidy**.
    a. neat
    b. dirty

13. Little Annie is very **bashful**.
    a. mean
    b. shy

14. Larry said that his wife was **amazed** by her present.
    a. surprised
    b. depressed

15. This room is extremely **large**.
    a. huge
    b. tiny

16. This fabric is very **soft**.
    a. rough
    b. smooth

17. I saw an apartment that was **disgusting**.
    a. dirty
    b. clean

Unit 9

Guided Conversation

1. apartment / tidy

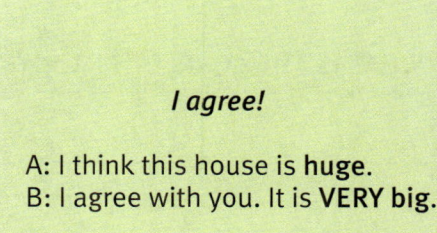

I agree!

A: I think this house is **huge**.
B: I agree with you. It is **VERY big**.

2. restaurant / fancy

3. movie / boring

4. class / great

5. museum / interesting

6. car / amazing

7. office / cluttered

8. answer / incorrect

9. candy / sweet

10. On your own.

Unit 9

Antonyms are words that mean the opposite

Exercise 9.6

Fill in the boxes.

WHAT IS THE CORRECT ANTONYM Of...?			
1. Long		2. Sweet	
3. Boring		4. Encouraging	
5. Tight		6. Useless	
7. Retail		8. Near	
9. Honest		10. Mean	
11. Shy		12. Slim	
13. Narrow		14. Neat	
15. Careful		16. Big	

Exercise 9.7

Read each sentence and fill in the blanks with the correct Antonym:

1. Ben isn't a careless driver, he is a _____ driver.
2. My friends aren't mean. They are_____.
3. My Math teacher isn't very boring. He is_____.
4. My room isn't very messy. It is extremely _____.
5. The food wasn't awful. It was very_____.
6. Susan hasn't been on time to work. She's been really_____.
7. Our house isn't small. It is quite_____.
8. I don't hate my mother in-law. I _____her.
9. Terry and Todd aren't polite all the time. Sometimes they're_____.
10. This lesson isn't so hard. It is pretty_____.
11. Barry doesn't have a temporary job. He has a _____job.
12. The floor is not dry. It is _____.

Unit 9

Exercise 9.8

Write the Antonym for each word.

Example: Young _____old_____

1. True _____
2. East _____
3. Good _____
4. Beautiful _____
5. Easy _____
6. Inside _____
7. Expensive _____
8. Beginning _____
9. Bottom _____
10. Cool _____
11. Fancy _____
12. Walk _____

Exercise 9.9

Rewrite each sentence using the Antonym of the underlined word.

Example: Millie ate the **terrible** food at the restaurant yesterday.
She ate the great food at the restaurant yesterday.

1. We've shown our **bad** homework to the teacher.
   _____.

2. My brother left his book **in front of** the classroom.
   _____.

3. Our children play in the park in the **summer**.
   _____.

4. I **fell asleep** at 11:00 PM last Monday night.
   _____.

5. Jennifer **found** her wallet at the airport a few weeks ago.
   _____.

6. Matthew was very **impolite** with his grandparents last night.
   _____.

7. This candy is not **sweet**, but we like it anyway.
   _____.

8. Italy had many **clean** roads in the outer city limits.
   _____.

Unit 9

Exercise 9.10

Match the following words with each correct Antonym:

1. _____ young
2. _____ borrow
3. _____ pull
4. _____ happy
5. _____ effect
6. _____ forget
7. _____ small
8. _____ full
9. _____ before
10. _____ north
11. _____ dry
12. _____ often

a. remember	b. cause
c. push	d. south
e. after	f. lend
g. empty	h. old
i. rarely	j. depressed
k. large	l. wet

Exercise 9.11

Write the Antonym for each underlined word in the paragraph.

Some people <u>love</u> to eat <u>certain</u> foods and others don't. In the United States, we have the <u>biggest</u> opportunity to try <u>different</u> kinds of foods from <u>many</u> different countries especially in "ethnic neighborhoods". For instance, in China Town, San Francisco, California, you and a <u>pal</u> can eat Chinese food. In Spanish Harlem, New York City, you can find Dominican or Puerto Rican food, and in <u>Little</u> Havana, Miami, Florida, you can <u>simply</u> get <u>some</u> Cuban food. In Iron Bound, Newark, New Jersey, you would <u>find</u> a restaurant that serves Portuguese food.

In most <u>cities</u> across the country, it wouldn't be <u>hard</u> to locate a neighborhood with the type of dishes you would enjoy. Do you know about any "ethnic neighborhoods" in your area?

1. *Love Hate*
2. _____.
3. _____.
4. _____.
5. _____.
6. _____.
7. _____.
8. _____.
9. _____.
10. _____.
11. _____.
12. _____.

Unit 9

Leaving the Comfort Zone

Reading

In life we run across two different kinds of people. We see the kind that are always very enthusiastic and are fun to be around, and the kind of people who are pessimistic and only see the negative side of things.

According to researchers, the optimistic enthusiast has a clear vision of what he wants in life and takes action in order to get there. On the other hand, the pessimist is satisfied with who he is, what he has and how he lives. Someone once said that the only way to change your life for the better is **"MAKING DECISIONS AND TAKING ACTION."** In other words, the best way to really accomplish things in life is by creating a mental picture of what we want and taking personal action with the purpose of getting there.

It is surprising to see how so many people are convinced that they do not have the power to change their lives. They feel terrified of leaving the "so-called" *comfort zone* they live in. They believe that they do not have what it takes to achieve things such as getting a better job, buying their dream home or simply going from obese to slender.

But, how can I achieve what I want by simply imagining it? Well, having a clear vision of our goals takes more than simply having a mental picture of it. It also represents changing the negative things around us that don't let us get to it.

It means writing a list of things that will help us accomplish the "primary goals" that are really important in our quest for success.

The road will not be an easy one, but the reward of finally conquering our fears and achieving our dreams will be worth all the effort.

Comprehension Sentences

1. What is the comfort zone?
2. Do you live in it?
3. Why are people afraid of leaving the comfort zone?
4. Discuss this phrase with your class. The best way to achieve things in life is by *making decisions and taking action*.

"I'm ready to accomplish all my goals."

Unit 9

Writing

A. Write a list of four people you know well in your class. Put their names in the following boxes and write three Synonyms (S) and three Antonyms (A) that best describe these people.

Example:

Name	Antonyms			Synonyms		
ROGER	tall	quiet	shy	friendly	thin	funny
MIKE	short	loud	outgoing	friendly	thin	funny

B. Talk about your friends.

Example:

- Roger is tall, but Mike is short.
- Mike is loud, but Roger is quiet.
- Mike is outgoing, but Roger is shy.
- Mike is friendly and so is Roger.
- Mike is thin and Roger is too.
- Roger is funny and so is Mike.

Name	Antonyms	Synonyms

UNIT 10

Content
- Tense Discrimination
- Tense Usage
- Review of Verbs

> *She **has worked** as a teacher for a long time*

01. COMMUNICATION   **02. COMPREHENSION**   **03. WRITING**   **04. GRAMMAR**

Unit 10

Never Judge a Book by Its Cover

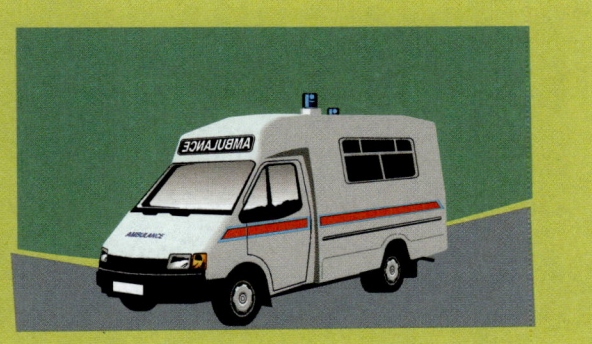

Reading

As a salesperson I have to travel from one town to another to show my products and visit prospective clients. My trips are generally very tiring and boring. I just sit behind the wheel and drive for miles and miles until I get to one town, then I visit my clients and stock them with my products. If it gets too late for me to get to the next town, I usually spend the night at a local motel since my wife doesn't like it when I drive at night or under bad weather conditions.

A couple of weeks ago, I experienced one of the hardest events anybody can go through. I had finished my work for the day, and since Greenville was the last town on my list I decided to head home. As I was about to leave the town, I looked at the time. It was six forty-five. It was kind of late. I said to myself, "If I drive as fast as permitted by the law, I will be home before midnight."

Suddenly, I remembered my wife's warning. I could picture her saying "Remember to spend the night wherever you are if it gets too late. I don't want anything bad to happen to you. The road can be very dangerous at night." I had just thought about that when I heard on a local radio station about a couple of bandits that had just robbed a nearby bank. They said that the thieves had escaped the police by stealing an ambulance that had gotten to the site to take some hurt people to the hospital.

The heavy rain and poor visibility made the scene even spookier. As I turned down a curve, I saw two people standing on the pouring rain. They were hitchhiking, and I still don't know why, but I pulled over to give them a ride. As soon as they got in the car, I immediately remembered my wife's words and the news I had recently heard on the radio. With my heart in my mouth, I saw an ambulance a couple of feet away. It had apparently had some kind of mechanical problem because it was in the middle of the road with the lights still on. The title of my story is "Never Judge a Book by Its Cover" let me explain to you why I gave it that title.

After talking to the couple for some time, I discovered that...

Comprehension Sentences

A. The story was written using different tenses: Simple Present Tense, Past Tense, etc. Find all the different tenses used in the story. Underline some sample sentences and share them with your class.

B. The story above doesn't have an ending. Sit in-groups and write a possible ending.

Unit 10

Grammar Focus

GRAMMAR TENSES REVIEW

SIMPLE PRESENT TENSE	PRESENT PROGRESSIVE TENSE
I *work* every day. He *works* every day.	Mary *is listening* to music now. They *are listening* to music.
SIMPLE PAST TENSE	**PAST PROGRESSIVE TENSE**
My parents *went* on vacation to Florida. Rita *saw* a good movie.	The children *were playing* with the dog. It *was raining* cats and dogs.
SIMPLE FUTURE TENSE	**FUTURE PROGRESSIVE TENSE**
Mark *will learn* how to dance. We *will be* here tomorrow.	I *will be studying* tomorrow at three. They *will be doing* their home work.
PRESENT PERFECT TENSE	**PRESENT PERFECT PROGRESSIVE**
I *have lived* in this town for five years. She *has worked* as a teacher for a long time.	She *has been teaching* for eight years. We *have been working* since 10:00 a.m.
PAST PERFECT TENSE	**PAST PERFECT PROGRESSIVE**
He *had gone* back to his country. Mark and Rita *had seen* that show.	I *had been eating* a lot of junk food. You *had been smoking* before I arrived.

Exercise 10.1

Tense discrimination. Look at these sentenses and identify the tense.

Example: John was sleeping. *Past Progressive Tense*

1. My siblings like to play video games ._____.
2. My friends have seen that play many times._____.
3. We will reveal the secret soon._____.
4. Janet had been on vacation. _____.
5. David and I were straightening the house. _____.
6. The president gave an interesting speech. _____.

Unit 10

7. I have been studying this language for a while. _____.
8. Mr. Barnes has a very modern car. _____.
9. My boss has traveled around the world. _____.
10. Jenny will be interviewing many people. _____.
11. It had been raining hard. _____.
12. Sarah has five children. _____.

Exercise 10.2

Questions & Negative sentences. Identify the correct tense.

> **Example:** Are you trying to make a phone call? *Present Progressive Tense*

1. Do you enjoy studying ESL? _____
2. You haven't paid the bills. _____
3. Will you be studying at 1:00? _____
4. It wasn't raining two hours ago. _____
5. Did you call me last night? _____
6. I'm not talking to you. _____
7. You don't have to pay the bills. _____
8. Has the president given the speech? _____
9. Had you watched that program? _____
10. You won't believe what happened. _____

Exercise 10.3

Complete the following conversation with the correct form of the verb in parenthesis:

> **Example:**
>
> A: What have you been doing?
> B: I *have been picking* apples. (pick)

168 | INTERACTIONS

Unit 10

1. A: John, what are you doing?
   B: I _____ my room. (clean up)

2. A: Sarah, what will you be doing at 11:00 am tomorrow morning?
   B: I _____ some e-mails to my clients. (write)

3. A: What had you been doing before we arrived?
   B: Well, I _____ for my final test. (study)

4. A: What do you enjoy doing in your spare time?
   B: I _____ around the park. (jog)

5. A: What was Raymond doing all day yesterday?
   B: He _____ his new sports car. (wash)

6. A: How long has Emilia been in this country?
   B: She _____ for about 8 years. (be)

7. A: What does Peter and Janet do on weekends?
   B: They _____ on field trips with their children. (go)

8. A: What did Mrs. Osaka do on the holiday?
   B: She _____ a new lamp for her family room. (buy)

9. A: What will the teacher do on his birthday?
   B: He _____ the day off and go on a picnic. (take)

10. A: Where had Henry gone before his girlfriend called him?
    B: He _____ to the basketball game with his friends. (go)

11. A: Why did Rita leave so early?
    B: She _____ early because she _____ a doctor's appointment. (leave/ have)

12. A: Where does Francis work?
    B: He _____ at an investment company in New York city. (work)

UNIT 10 | 169

Unit 10

Exercise 10.4

Verb tense. Complete the following sentences with the correct form of the verb.

1. Angela and I _____ shopping last night. (go)
2. Robert _____ in this country for 3 years. (be)
3. Mr. and Mrs. Morgan _____ in a beautiful village. (live)
4. Our landlord _____ the door knobs next week. (change)
5. By the time we _____ (arrive) at the party, everyone _____. (leave)
6. Thelma _____ letters since 10:00 this morning. (write)
7. The children _____ their homework right now. (do)
8. Betty _____ in the shower when I opened the door. (sing)
9. We _____ on this exercise for 10 minutes. (work)
10. Look outside! It _____. (snow)
11. I am so tired this morning. I _____ up until very late last night. (stay)
12. When our boss _____ (arrive), we _____. (laugh)

Exercise 10.5

Oral exercise. Answer the following questions:

1. What will you be doing at 9:00 a.m. tomorrow morning?
2. How many hours did you work yesterday?
3. What time do you usually get up?
4. What were you doing at 7:00 p.m. last night?
5. What is your current address? How long have you lived there?
6. Where do you work? How long have you worked there?
7. How long have you been studying English as a second language?
8. Look at your teacher, what is he/she doing right now?
9. Before the teacher arrived in the classroom, what had been you been doing?
10. Why are you studying this language?
11. What will you do this weekend?
12. How long have we been doing this exercise?

What did you do then?
What are you doing now?
What will you do next?

Reading

When I was little, my parents taught me to be discreet and told me not to ask people too many questions. They said that people don't like it when others get into their business. Now that I am a grownup, I understand why they said so. Even though I agree with them, I can't stop asking people questions because I happen to be the host for a radio show where I have to interview people all the time.

CONVERSATION #1

Caller 1: Hello. Is this KWTYZ?

Host: Yes, it is. Thank you for calling. Who am I speaking to?

Caller 1: Hi! This is Sandra Thomas. I am calling to ask you to play my favorite song.

Host: Yes, of course. But first, I have to ask you a few questions if that is OK.

Caller 1: Sure! What do you want to know?

Host: Where were you born?

Caller 1: I was born in Orlando, Florida.

Host: What do you do for a living?

Caller 1: Well, I am currently unemployed.

Host: What is your favorite song?

Caller: It is "Now That I Don't Have You" by George Benson.

Host: And what is the best radio station in town?

Caller 1: It is KWTYZ of course!

Host: Here is your song, and thank you for calling.

Unit 10

CONVERSATION # 2

Caller 2: Hi! I am calling to find out about the free backstage passes to the Green Turtles Concert.

Host: Sure. All you have to do to participate is answer a few very simple questions.

Caller 2: OK. I am ready.

Host: The first question is: When was I, your friend and host Robert "Friendly Bob" Rogers, born?

Caller: Oh! I surely know this one. You were born on January 21, 1972.

Host: Perfect answer! When did I become a radio host?

Caller 2: You became a radio host in 1995.

Host: Excellent! Well, I guess you know everything about me. Let's see. One final question: Am I married? If yes, how long have I been married?

Caller 2: Yes, you are. You have been married for over ten years. Eleven, to be precise.

Host: Wow. I guess we have a winner! Congratulations! Now stay on the line, and I will tell you where you can pick up your tickets.

Caller 2: Thank you so much. I love listening to KWTYZ.

Comprehension Sentences

A. Underline and identify all different grammar tenses in the conversations.

B. Write some of sentences you underlined in the space provided and the grammar tense in the parentheses.

| Example: | _When I was little_ (simple past tense) |

1. _____ (......................)
2. _____ (......................)
3. _____ (......................)
4. _____ (......................)
5. _____ (......................)
6. _____ (......................)
7. _____ (......................)
8. _____ (......................)
9. _____ (......................)
10. _____ (......................)

C. Write another telephone conversation like the ones above. Use your imagination as well as different grammar tenses.

Exercise 10.6

Verb Tenses. Change the following sentences to the negative form.

Example:
Kyan took the bus yesterday.
He didn't take the bus yesterday

1. Mr. Robinson works for an important law firm.
   _____.

2. Gary and Jerry have to work overtime tomorrow.
   _____.

3. James and Peter have worked at the County Jail for two years.
   _____.

4. The police officer gave me a speeding ticket.
   _____.

5. Henry is having a dinner party this evening.
   _____.

6. The school meeting will be held at 3:00 p.m.
   _____.

7. Jennifer has an extended family.
   _____.

8. Ms. Meyers has written classified ads for many years.
   _____.

9. I have to send some money to my brother in college.
   _____.

10. Samantha does her homework every day.
    _____.

11. We had seen that movie before.
    _____.

12. My in-laws were remodeling their house.
    _____.

Unit 10

Exercise 10.7

Verb Tenses. Change the following sentences to Questions.

| Example : | The bell is ringing. |
| | *Is the bell ringing?* |

1. Fiona speaks four languages fluently.
   _____.

2. My co-workers will be having a picnic.
   _____.

3. The bus passed by at 9:30 pm.
   _____.

4. Our stepfather has purchased a new boat.
   _____.

5. Sally has read many books lately.
   _____.

6. Martha has to read two books this semester.
   _____.

7. The office has an astounding view.
   _____.

8. The kids are doing their homework.
   _____.

9. My aunt won the lottery last month.
   _____.

10. They had traveled to Europe before.
    _____.

11. My best friend was having surgery.
    _____.

12. My classmates and I need to study for the test.
    _____.

Unit 10

Exercise 10.8

Oral exercise. Verb Tenses. Give short affirmative answers to the following questions, then practice with a partner.

| Example: | Do you want to go camping? |
| | Yes, I do. |

1. Will you be leaving soon?
2. Were you in class yesterday?
3. Did you see the new movie?
4. Does Ralph work on Sundays?
5. Is it raining now?
6. Are you willing to do your best?
7. Has Betty arrived yet?
8. Does Linda have children?
9. Was I talking three minutes ago?
10. Have Bob and Peter been interviewed?
11. Will you come to class every day?
12. Had John arrived before I called?
13. Did you learn the past participles by heart?
14. Am I tall enough to play basketball?
15. Have I ever lied to you?

Exercise 10.9

Verb tenses. Give negative short answers to the following questions, then practice with a partner.

| Example: | Does Richard work a lot? |
| | No, he doesn't. |

1. Are you mean to others?
2. Was Peter working at 10:00?
3. Were you taking a nap ten minutes ago?
4. Did you do your homework assignment?
5. Have you ever seen a UFO?
6. Has it snowed lately?
7. Will you marry me?
8. Does your brother take the bus?
9. Has Linda ever given a speech?
10. Had Edward gone to bed when his girlfriend called?
11. Had you studied English before you came to this country?
12. Did you prepare a romantic dinner for your significant other?
13. Will you be studying English five years from now?
14. Am I a pessimistic?
15. Was I late for the lecture?

Unit 10

Exercise 10.10

Information Questions. Verb Tenses. Make questions with the words you have in parenthesis. Pay special attention to the Structure

> **Example:** - Janet had a party last week. (When)
> *When did she have a party?*

1. Janet and Robert are fixing their house. (What)
   _____?

2. The Johnsons were on vacation last week. (When)
   _____?

3. Betty had done the dishes before I arrived. (What)
   _____?

4. The children went to the zoo last month. (Where)
   _____?

5. David has been in this country for three years. (How long)
   _____?

6. The building was destroyed by fire. (How)
   _____?

7. Dr. Monty will be seeing Ms. Benns tomorrow. (Who)
   _____?

8. Victor left because he had something to do. (Why)
   _____?

9. James works at a Demolition Company. (Where)
   _____?

10. I am leaving at 3:00 pm today. (What time)
    _____?

11. I have done many things. (What)
    _____?

12. I have two children. (How many)
    _____?

176 | INTERACTIONS

Unit 10

Guided Conversation

What do you do for a living?

A: Who's that?
B: *That's Mr. Peterson.*
A: What does he do for living?
B: *He is a doctor.*
A: How long has he been a doctor?
B: *He's been a doctor since 1998.*

1. Ms. Myers / nurse / 1999.

2. Robert / mechanic / 7 years.

3. Janet / cashier / a long time.

4. Mr. Reynolds / janitor / a while.

5. Becky / cheerleader / last year.

6. Mrs. Peters / mail carrier / ten years.

7. Nick / salesman / April.

8. Rosario / telemarketer / 3 years.

9. Mr. Bush / accountant / years.

10. On your own.

Unit 10

Exercise 10.11

Look at the pictures and create conversation based on the situation you see. Work with a partner.

A: _____
B: _____
A: _____
B: _____
A: _____
B: _____
A: _____

A: _____
B: _____
A: _____
B: _____
A: _____
B: _____
A: _____

A: _____
B: _____
A: _____
B: _____
A: _____
B: _____
A: _____

A: _____
B: _____
A: _____
B: _____
A: _____
B: _____
A: _____

178 | INTERACTIONS

Good, better, best. Never let it rest until the good is better and the better is best.

Unit 10

Reading

My friends and English teacher are really impressed with my progress. Even though I have studied English for only six months, they think I am doing very well. In fact, here is a letter I sent to my parents a few days ago. I know I still have to improve. My letter has some mistakes that I want you to help me correct. Please rewrite it in the space provided and thank you for your help.

Dear Parents,

I know it have been more than three weeks since I last wrote to you. I must say I have been very busy studying for my finals. I want you to know that I really missing you and wish you could being here with you.

Well. Let me tell you that many good things have happened in the last few weeks. First of all, I go to a wonderful party last weekend. A lot of friends from my school was there and we had a wonderful time together. They taught me how to dance to American music and I also eat a lot of traditional American food such as meat loaf and potato salad.

I has to admit that I really miss you, but I also understand that the sacrifice I am making will pay off in the end. I really wants to learn about the American culture and to be able to communicate in English with my friends and classmates.

My English teacher tell me that my English have improved a lot, and that my writing is getting better and better.

I promise to write more often and I hope that you did it too. I can't wait for Christmas to come so that you can finally visit me. My host family really want to meet you and I just can't wait to introduce you to my friends.

I love you and misses you a lot.

Your son,

Manuel

Unit 10

Writing

A. Look at the letter on the previous page. Write the letter again and make sure you correct all the mistakes.

Dear parents:

_____

_____

_____

_____

_____

_____

_____

_____

_____

_____

_____

_____

_____

_____

_____

_____

_____

_____

_____

Your son,

Manuel

Irregular Verbs

Appendix 1

	Base Form	Simple Past	Past Participle
1.	arise	arose	arisen
2.	abide	abode	abode/abided
3.	awake	awoke/awoken	awoke/awoken
4.	be	was/were	been
5.	bear	bore	borne
6.	beat	beat	beaten/beat
7.	befall	befell	befallen
8.	beget	begot	begotten
9.	become	became	become
10.	begin	began	begun
11.	behold	beheld	beheld
12.	bend	bent	bent
13.	bereave	bereaved	bereft
14.	beseech	beseeched	besought
15.	beset	beset	beset
16.	bet	bet	bet
17.	bid	bid	bid
18.	bite	bit	bitten
19.	bleed	bled	bled
20.	blow	blew	blown
21.	break	broke	broken
22.	breed	bred	bred
23.	bring	brought	brought
24.	broadcast	broadcast/ed	broadcast/ed
25.	build	built	built
26.	burn	burned/burnt	burned/burnt
27.	burst	burst	burst
28.	buy	bought	bought
29.	cast	cast	cast
30.	can	could	--------
31.	catch	caught	caught
32.	chide	chided	chiden
33.	choose	chose	chosen
34.	cleave	cleaved	cloven
35.	cling	clung	clung
36.	come	came	come
37.	cost	cost	cost
38.	creep	crept	crept
39.	cut	cut	cut
40.	crow	crew	crowed
41.	deal	dealt	dealt
42.	dig	dug	dug
43.	dive	dive/dove	dived
44.	do	did	done
45.	draw	drew	drawn

Appendix 1 — Irregular Verbs

	Base Form	Simple Past	Past Participle
46.	dream	dreamed/dreamt	dreamed/dreamt
47.	drink	drank	drunk
48.	drive	drove	driven
49.	dwell	dwelled	dwelt
50.	eat	ate	eaten
51.	fall	fell	fallen
52.	feed	fed	fed
53.	feel	felt	felt
54.	fight	fought	fought
55.	find	found	found
56.	fit	fit	fit
57.	flee	fled	fled
58.	fling	flung	flung
59.	fly	flew	flown
60.	forbid	forbade/forbad	forbidden/forbid
61.	forbear	forbore	forborne
62.	foresee	foresaw	foreseen
63.	foretell	foretold	foretold
64.	forget	forgot	forgotten
65.	forgive	forgave	forgiven
66.	forsake	forsook	forsaken
67.	forgo	forwent	forgone
68.	freeze	froze	frozen
69.	get	got	gotten/got
70.	gild	gilded	gilt
71.	gird	girded	girt
72.	give	gave	given
73.	go	went	gone
74.	grind	ground	ground
75.	grow	grew	grown
76.	hang	hung	hung
77.	have	had	had
78.	hear	heard	heard
79.	heave	heaved	hove
80.	hew	hewed	hewn
81.	hide	hid	hidden
82.	hit	hit	hit
83.	hold	held	held
84.	hurt	hurt	hurt
85.	inlay	inlaid	inlaid
86.	keep	kept	kept
87.	kneel	knelt/kneeled	knelt/kneeled
88.	knit	knit/knitted	knit/knitted
89.	know	knew	known
90.	lay	laid	laid

Irregular Verbs

Appendix 1

	Base Form	Simple Past	Past Participle
91.	lead	led	led
92.	leap	leaped/leapt	leaped/leapt
93.	leave	left	left
94.	lend	lent	lent
95.	let	let	let
96.	lie (down)	lay	lain
97.	light	lit	lit
98.	lose	lost	lost
99.	make	made	made
100.	may	might	--------
101.	mow	mowed	mowed
102.	must	--------	--------
103.	mean	meant	meant
104.	meet	met	met
105.	melt	melted	melted
106.	mislead	misled	misled
107.	mistake	mistook	mistaken
108.	misunderstand	misunderstood	misunderstood
109.	ought	ought	--------
110.	outdo	outdid	outdone
111.	overcome	overcame	overcome
112.	pay	paid	paid
113.	partake	partook	partaken
114.	put	put	put
115.	prove	proved	proved/proven
116.	quit	quit	quit
117.	read	read	read
118.	rid	rid/ridded	rid/ridded
119.	ride	rode	ridden
120.	ring	rang	rung
121.	rise	rose	risen
122.	run	ran	run
123.	saw	sawed	sawed/sawn
124.	say	said	said
125.	see	saw	seen
126.	seek	sought	sought
127.	sell	sold	sold
128.	send	sent	sent
129.	set	set	set
130.	sew	sewed	sewed/sewn
131.	shake	shook	shaken
132.	shall	should	--------
133.	shave	shaved	shaved/shaved
134.	shear	sheared	sheared/shorn
135.	shine	shone/shined	shone/shined

Appendix 1 — Irregular Verbs

	Base Form	Simple Past	Past Participle
136.	shoot	shot	shot
137.	shoe	shod	shod
138.	show	showed	showed/shown
139.	shrink	shrank/shrunk	shrunk/shrunked
140.	shut	shut	shut
141.	sing	sang	sung
142.	sink	sank	sunk
143.	sit	sat	sat
144.	slay	slew	slain
145.	sleep	slept	slept
146.	slide	slid	slid
147.	sling	slung	slung
148.	slink	slunk	slunk
149.	slit	slit	slit
150.	smite	smote	smitten
151.	sow	sowed	sown
152.	sneak	sneaked/snuck	sneaked/snuck
153.	speak	spoke	spoken
154.	speed	speeded/sped	speeded/sped
155.	spend	spent	spent
156.	spill	spilled/spilt	spilled/spilt
157.	spin	spun	spun
158.	spit	spat/spit	spat/spit
159.	split	split	split
160.	spread	spread	spread
161.	spring	sprang/sprung	sprung
162.	stand	stood	stood
163.	steal	stole	stolen
164.	stick	stuck	stuck
165.	sting	stung	stung
166.	stink	stank/stunk	stunk
167.	strew	strewed	strewn
168.	stride	strode	stridden
169.	strive	strived	striven
170.	strike	struck	struck/strike
171.	swear	swore	sworn
172.	sweep	swept	swept
173.	swell	swelled	swelled/swollen
174.	swim	swam	swum
175.	swing	swung	swung
176.	take	took	taken
177.	teach	taught	taught
178.	tear	tore	torn
179.	tell	told	told
180.	think	thought	thought

Irregular Verbs

Base Form	Simple Past	Past Participle
181. throw	threw	thrown
182. thrive	throve	thriven
183. thrust	thrust	thrust
184. tread	trod	trodden
185. undergo	underwent	undergone
186. understand	understood	understood
187. undertake	undertook	undertaken
188. undo	undid	undone
189. uphold	upheld	upheld
190. upset	upset	upset
191. wake	woke/waked	waked/woken
192. wear	wore	worn
193. weave	wove/weaved	woven/weaven
194. weep	wept	wept
195. wed	wedded	wed
196. win	won	won
197. write	wrote	written
198. withdraw	withdrew	withdrawn
199. withstand	withstood	withstood
200. wet	wet/wetted	wet

Appendix 2 — Phrasal Verbs

COMMON SEPARABLE PHRASAL VERBS

1.	Ask out	ask someone to go on a date
2.	Ask over	invite to one's house
3.	Bloch out	stop from passing through.
4.	Blow out	stop burning by blowing on it
5.	Blow up	make explode
6.	Bring about	make happen
7.	Bring back	return
8.	Bring down	depress
9.	Bring out	introduce (a new product/book)
10.	Bring up	raise (a child)
11.	Burn down	burn completely
12.	Call back	return a telephone call
13.	Call in	ask for help with a problem
14.	Call off	cancel
15.	Call up	make a telephone call
16.	Carry out	conduct (a plan/experiment)
17.	Cross out	draw a line through
18.	Charge up	charge with electricity
19.	Cheer up	cause to feel happier
20.	Clean up	clean completely
21.	Close down	close by force
22.	Cover up	cover completely
23.	Cut down	bring down by cutting (a tree)
24.	Cut off	stop the supply of
25.	Cut out	remove by cutting
26.	Do over	do again
27.	Do up	make more beautiful
28.	Draw together	unite
29.	Dream up	invent
30.	Drink up	drink completely
31.	Drop off	leave something / someone someplace
32.	Empty out	empty completely
33.	Figure out	understand (after thinking about)
34.	Fill in	complete the sentence by writing in a blank
35.	Fill out	complete (a form)
36.	Fill up	fill completely
37.	Find out	discover information
38.	Get across	get people to understand an idea
39.	Give away	give without charging money
40.	Give back	return
41.	Give out	distribute
42.	Give up	quit, abandon

Phrasal Verbs

COMMON SEPARABLE PHRASAL VERBS

43.	Hand in	submit work (to a boss/teacher)
44.	Hand out	distribute
45.	Help out	assist
46.	Hang up	put on a hook or hanger
47.	Hold on	keep attached
48.	Lay off	end employment
49.	Lay out	arrange according to a plan
50.	Leave on	not turn off (a radio/a light)
51.	Leave out	omit
52.	Let down	disappoint
53.	Let in	allow to enter
54.	Let off	allow to leave (a bus/a car)
55.	Let out	allow to leave
56.	Light up	illuminate
57.	Look over	examine
58.	Look up	try to find information in a reference book
59.	Make up	create
60.	Move around	change the location
61.	Pass out	distribute
62.	Pass up	decide not to use
63.	Pay back	repay
64.	Pick out	select
65.	Pick up	lift
66.	Point out	indicate
67.	Put away	put in an appropriate place
68.	Put back	return to its original place
69.	Put off	postpone
70.	Put down	stop holding or carrying
71.	Start over	start again
72.	Shut off	stop (a machine/light)
73.	Straighten up	make neat
74.	Switch on	start (a machine/light)
75.	Take away	remove
76.	Take back	return
77.	Take in	notice, understand, and remember
78.	Take off	remove (clothes)
79.	Talk over	discuss
80.	Tear down	destroy
81.	Tear up	tear into small pieces
82.	Tear off	detach
83.	Think over	consider
84.	Think up	invent

Appendix 2 — Phrasal Verbs

COMMON SEPARABLE PHRASAL VERBS

#	Phrasal Verb	Meaning
85.	Throw away	discard
86.	Throw out	put in the trash
87.	Try on	put clothing to see if it fits
88.	Turn on	start (a machine/light)
89.	Turn off	stop (a machine/light)
90.	Turn over	turn something so the top side is at the bottom
91.	Turn up	raise the volume
92.	Use up	use completely
93.	Wake up	awaken
94.	Work off	remove by work or activity
95.	Work out	solve
96.	Write down	write on a piece of paper
97.	Write up	write in a finished form

COMMON NON SEPARABLE PHRASAL VERBS

#	Phrasal Verb	Meaning
1.	Carry on	continue
2.	Come off	become unattached
3.	Come up with	invent
4.	Count on	depend on
5.	Drop out of	quit
6.	Follow through with	complete
7.	Get out of	leave (a car/taxi)
8.	Get back (from)	return from a trip
9.	Get in	enter (a car/taxi)
10.	Get off	leave (a bus/plane/train/bicycle)
11.	Get over	recover from an illness
12.	Get out of	leave (a car/taxi)
13.	Get through (with)	finish
14.	Get along (with)	good relationship with
15.	Go after	pursue
16.	Go along with	support
17.	Keep up with	go as fast as
18.	Keep on	continue
19.	Look out (for)	be careful
20.	Run into	meet accidentally
21.	Run out of	finish the supply of something
22.	Stick with/to	not quit, not leave
23.	Team up with	start to work with
24.	Think back on	remember
25.	Turn around	change the direction
26.	Watch out (for)	be careful

Gerunds and Infinitives

Appendix 3

COMMON VERBS FOLLOWED BY A GERUND

Acknowledge	Deny	Feel like	Mind	Regret
Admit	Detest	Finish	Postpone	Report
Advise	Discontinue	Forgive	Practice	Resent
Appreciate	Discuss	Give Up	Prevent	Resist
Avoid	Dislike	Imagine	Prohibit	Risk
Can't Help	Endure	Justify	Propose	Suggest
Celebrate	Enjoy	Keep	Quit	Support
Consider	Escape	Mention	Recall	Tolerate
Delay	Explain	Miss	Recommend	Understand

COMMON VERBS FOLLOWED BY AN INFINITIVE

Afford	Choose	Hope	Offer	Struggle
Agree	Consent	Hurry	Pay	Swear
Appear	Decide	Intend	Plan	Volunteer
Arrange	Deserve	Learn	Prepare	Wait
Ask	Expect	Manage	Pretend	Want
Attempt	Fail	Mean	Promise	Wish
Can't Afford	Grow	Need	Refuse	Would Like
Can't Wait	Help	Neglect	Request	Yearn
	Hesitate		Seem	

COMMON VERBS FOLLOWED BY AN INFINITIVE OR GERUND

Begin	Forget*	Like	Start
Can't Stand	Hate	Prefer	Stop*
Continue	Love	Remember*	Try*

*These verbs can be followed by either a gerund or infinitive but there is a big difference in meaning.